A Fast Bike Through the Badlands

Andy C Wareing

Andy C Wareing

Copyright © 2024 Andy C Wareing All rights reserved

No part of this book may be reproduced, or stored in a retrieval system, or transmitted in any form or by any means, electronic, mechanical, photocopying, recording, or otherwise, without express written permission of the publisher.

Cover design by Andy C Wareing

All rights reserved.

Contents

1. Serendipity — 1
2. A First Farewell — 7
3. A Plan Comes Together — 15
4. Off With a Wobble — 21
5. Talladega — 36
6. Muscle Shoals — 47
7. Civil War — 60
8. The Sunset Motel — 79
9. Pass In Review — 95
10. Des Moines — 100
11. Badlands — 108
12. Fargo — 127

13.	What Bike!	139
14.	San Diego	146
15.	Kingman	167
16.	Grand Canyon	181
17.	Prescott	192
18.	Tucson	204
19.	Mexico	214
20.	Germany?	225
21.	Galveston	233
22.	Piggly Wiggly	242
23.	Pensacola	253
24.	Another Farewell	275
	Andy C Wareing	293

Serendipity

Unlike Micky Dolenz and the rest of The Monkees, I have never been much of a believer.

Not for a single moment a believer in some all-powerful, all-seeing type of God. Not in karma, or destiny, not in kismet, the stars, predestination, or fate. Certainly not a believer in mystic readings, palms or the tarot, or an eternity with relatives, sat on some fluffy cloud beyond the great mysterious veil.

I am as likely to believe in astrology as much as I will ever believe in flying reindeers at Christmas or why we have a bunny that brings chocolate eggs as a gift for Jesus at Easter.

But then there is serendipity.

Serendipity is both a word and a concept I can get behind.

Serendipity doesn't rely on supernatural movers or phenomena. It is just a happy accident, a simple coincidence. A roll of the dice. But one that favours the fortunes of the individuals it graces in some manner.

And so it was that, completely unlooked for, I found myself stepping down from the sterile safety of the sidewalk and into the fast-moving path of the serendipity express.

It all took place during a random conversation at a neighbour's house, one sunny afternoon during my last few months of living in the United States.

My neighbour of a few doors down had owned motorcycles ever since we had moved into the large subdivision in Roswell Georgia we had chosen to call home. When he found out I was an old biker myself, we had made an easy friendship. He wanted me to buy a bike so we could go ride together but I was very reluctant. The roads in Atlanta, where we lived at the time, were notoriously busy and dangerous. Most drivers in Atlanta are poorly equipped in both a sensory and motor skills capacity to safely venture on simple expeditions to the shops, never mind dealing with, and avoiding, the sending of speeding motorcyclists to the repair shop, the casualty department, or the morgue.

Every car in a twenty-mile radius of the city bore a prang and a scrape from a previous encounter with something either moving or often, simply stationary. At times I still craved a motorcycle, I guess it was deeply entwined within some errant helix strand of my DNA, but the traffic around us was generally more hazardous than being blind drunk, while seated backwards on a moped, riding in the wrong direction around a busy demolition derby circuit.

We had popped across to the neighbour's house one afternoon, for a birthday or other mildly dull social event, and with a few beers in hand me and my neighbour friend had escaped the festivities to do what we always did, to stand in his spacious garage, generally talking shit, and looking at, and playing with, his trucks and bike.

My neighbour had owned a Hayabusa when we first moved in and now, he had a smart little Ducati Scrambler safely ensconced in his man cave. The Scrambler was pretty, and I was quite envious of it. It looked easy to ride, low slung, powerful, and fun. I sat astride the bike while we chatted, idly playing with the controls, and generally making sure that the next time he started it up, the bike's high beam and hazards would be on, and it would be in third gear.

In our conversation I was surprised to find out that he had just sold the Ducati, to somebody on eBay. He wanted another Hayabusa. Now he needed to make plans to ship the Ducati from Atlanta all the way north, to Fargo in very distant North Dakota. What my neighbour had not considered was the not inconsiderable price of shipping such a commodity across close to 1,500 miles before accepting the bid.

Normally of course, I would have just taken the piss, and wet myself laughing at the silly predicament he had got himself into.

Perhaps it was the two or three light domestic beers talking, or the familiar feel of, once more, being sat on a motorcycle, but all of a sudden, I found myself coming up with the brilliant idea of how he could save on the delivery fees.

If, instead of paying for a professional courier, he would let me ride the bike north and deliver the Ducati to the new owner on his behalf, he could save the few hundred bucks it was going to cost him. I would even pay for the petrol myself. Without pausing to consider the logistics of such an endeavour, or, perhaps more crucially, what my wife might think of such a proposal, my mouth began to form the words.

The much more sane and sober side of me sat quietly askance while he listened to the much more foolish and slightly inebriated part of me explain my idea to my immediately interested neighbour.

Suddenly my hand was pumped, and plans were drawn. My neighbour reached for his cell phone and immediately checked with the buyer of the bike if he minded a few extra miles on the clock in exchange for a bespoke, careful, and entirely personalized doorstep delivery.

As I began to sober a little, I began to ponder exactly how far Fargo could be from Atlanta, and started to fervently hope that the extra mileage would be a deal breaker, but the eager young man on the other end of the cell phone readily agreed.

Rat's cocks!

Later that day, a touch nervously, I admitted my blunder and discussed my unexpected dilemma with Paula.

To my surprise she was startlingly supportive. I guess that in my youth, when she had first met me, when I had attempted in my own awkward way to woo her (is that still even a word?), I had always been quite the impulsive and reckless adventurer. The risk taker, the spontaneously idiotic friend that people kept around solely for entertainment reasons. I guess that at least some of those qualities must have attracted her to the otherwise skinny, prematurely balding, knobhead that I surely was.

But I couldn't deny that recently some of that laissez-fair and cavalier approach to life—that let's go to Marrakesh tomorrow spirit—had been replaced by a rather dull and serious man neither of us entirely recognized.

We looked at the map together and realized that we might even be able to kill a couple of birds with this single motorized stone that had been pushed unexpectedly into our hands.

A First Farewell

A time was fast approaching when we would have to begin to say our farewells to the United States.

Farewell to this fascinatingly enthralling, endlessly braggadocios, ridiculously insular, deliciously compelling, and, at the same time, maddeningly foreign country we had grown to love. Farewell to our friends, our neighbours, the unfamiliar places that we had slowly worked hard to make familiar. The places where we had laboured hard to eke out a comfortable and happy life for ourselves.

It would soon be goodbye to buffalo wings and ranch sauce, so long to footlongs, sayonara to sushi, bon voyage to burgers as big as our heads and tootle pip to the innumerable rare and succulent tomahawk steaks that had contributed to giving me gold medal winning, record breaking numbers in the blood pressure and cholesterol games.

But also farewell to our eldest son. Ben was about to leave us. To join the United States Navy and an almost immediate posting to Japan, carried there on the U.S.S Ronald Reagan aircraft carrier that was returning home to play its defensive role along the Pacific Rim.

It was upsetting for my wife Paula and myself to suddenly realize we had arrived so unexpectedly at the life stage where we had to let him go. To let him grow to become who he was destined to be. The first of our scruffy baby birds to leave the nest.

Ben had recently graduated high school and secured a place at Kennesaw State University to study math. But only a few days before we had to pay the college fees, he had pulled out. We had the usual parent-child discussion about his decision, in that we had yelled and gesticulated at each other for ten minutes or so.

He then told me that he wanted to enjoy a gap year and take a year off school.

After I got back to my feet and dried the tears of hilarity from my ruddy cheeks, I patiently explained to him that sitting in my basement, smoking dope and playing the Xbox for a year was about as likely to happen as me ever enjoying the music of Cliff Richards or the movie adaptation of the musical Cats.

Ten minutes later we were seated in the car together driving down the Atlanta Highway, heading towards the military recruiting centres that were all clustered together in an inauspicious looking group of buildings opposite the Longhorn Steakhouse on Mansell Road.

We had first strolled across to look in the window of the recruiting centre for the US Marines. The poster showed some tough looking guy with narrowed eyes, covered in somebody else's blood, with the strapline '*First to Fight*' scrawled underneath. We looked at each other and both shook our heads in unison.

Next to the Marines was the US Army recruiting office. In this window was a poster depicting a harried looking young man, holding onto his helmet while cowering in a mud filled foxhole with ordnance exploding overhead. Again, another synchronised shake of the head.

The last recruiting office on the block was the one for the US Navy. The poster in this window depicted a sleek looking destroyer ploughing with ease through an azure sea. Helicopters buzzed around in the air above the ship and a row of white dressed sailors stood to attention, smiling gleefully on the pristine deck. The bell on the door rang as we walked in.

Thirty minutes later a pile of forms signed in triplicate stood precariously balanced on the desk of the eager recruiting officer. We all shook hands and set off for home to await the joining up papers to arrive.

At the same time that Ben signed the next four years of his life away and took the first tentative steps towards the very beginning of his career, I found myself inching toward the end of mine. I was beginning to plan an early retirement. A way to separate myself from the stress and hubbub of corporate software sales.

We didn't know what we were going to do with our new lives yet. But there was a strong rumour circulating of a new location, a different country, one dappled by Mediterranean sunshine filtering through the fragranced petals of a bougainvillea perhaps. A life filled with long lazy days, where the slow passing of time was marked only by the sound of clinking ice in a glass and the glug of another cerveza being poured.

Fifteen years in the United States had flitted by. We had become citizens, and were privileged enough to have travelled extensively, but suddenly there were a thousand places I realized that I hadn't managed to see or visit. Whatever our final plan turned out to be, we still had a decent amount of time left in the states, and some time to kill before we even began to start thinking about tidying the house ready for placing it on the market.

At work, word had inevitably got around that I was about to throw in the towel. I had already handed over many of my day-to-day work duties to a colleague and now, largely ignored and dropped from an exponentially increasing number of meeting invites, I was, for a while, content in kicking my feet and cashing the checks.

In those long and suddenly idle days I would spend my time staring at the giant map of the United States I had hung on the wall behind my desk at home. I had put the map on the wall fifteen years ago when we had first moved to the USA and my wife, Paula, had stuck a shiny cardboard arrow on the map, its tip pointing to Atlanta. She had helpfully written, "*you are here*," on it to help me out a little as I slowly became familiar with US geography.

Ben's joining up papers arrived only the day before I had the booze fuelled conversation with my neighbour about delivering the Scrambler. Ben was starting his Navy bootcamp at the Great Lakes Naval Station in just a few weeks. Great Lakes is situated north of Chicago and only two days ride away from where I needed to be in order to deliver the Ducati Scrambler in the city of Fargo, located in very far away North Dakota. More serendipity.

If I set off on my way north, I could visit a few of the things and places I had always wanted to see En-route and meet Paula north of Chicago in time to see Ben graduate. I could then see her off back to the airport and continue on my way to Fargo to drop the Ducati off.

A few short weeks later we had a farewell party for Ben at the house in Roswell. It was a small affair, just some neighbours, a few of our close friends and two of Ben's best buddies.

The next day we drove Ben to a hotel close to Atlanta airport. He looked pale and nervous with his few possessions. The lobby was full of identical looking young men and women sporting new buzz cuts. They were all spending their last night as civilians before the bus picked them up the next morning to transport them to Hartsfield-Jackson airport and the onward flight to Chicago, where they would spend ten weeks in bootcamp before, hopefully, graduating as Navy sailors.

Ben checked in to the hotel and stored his stuff in a shared bedroom and we took him out for one final dinner as a family. It was a very sombre affair in what turned out to be a horrendously busy Outback restaurant. The booths were filled with anxious teenagers and worried looking parents all doing the same thing that we were doing.

We were all there trying to forget that tomorrow we would all be parted from our kids. It didn't help that every now and again the building shook as a Delta airliner, on final approach, roared low over the roof of the restaurant, reminding us all of the airport that loomed close by, a constant promise of a future severance.

We ate mostly in silence. I was worried about my son. I knew deep down, intellectually, that he would be just fine. He may have been angry, and sulky in his day-to-day interactions with me, but he was charming, funny, and likeable with almost everybody else. He also knew his own mind well and wasn't afraid or averse to backing that up with a heavy fist or two if pushed too far.

Ben would muddle through whatever hardships and challenges the Navy could muster. He was built for the military. But, at the same time, this boy who drove me completely insane had never been parted from us for more than a day or two, and now we would have absolutely no contact with him, other than an occasional old school handwritten letter, for ten long weeks.

After dinner we drove him back to the hotel and, in the car park, we said our final farewells. I knew that deep down he was seriously apprehensive and frightened because, for the first time in nearly ten years he wrapped his arms tight around me and hugged me. He was already two inches taller than me and several pounds heavier. He squeezed me so hard it made my eyes water a little.

"I love you Dad," he whispered.

"I love you too Benjy," I managed. A croak. A voice strangled taut by emotion. "Be good. Be safe. See you in a few weeks, OK?"

Silence. He turned.

And then...my boy was gone.

A Plan Comes Together

The Xbox in the basement, usually white hot with play, sat abandoned.

The room where Ben had spent all of his spare time felt alien and uncomfortable. It gave me that slightly bowel liquifying feeling when you find yourself in somebody else's house when you really shouldn't be there — and don't ask me how I know that feeling so well.

Still, it had been many years since I had had the chance to play the Xbox myself, so I took the opportunity to play a quick game of Tom Clancy's Rainbow Six. It was one of Ben's favourites and one he made look easy. I was quietly confident I would be good at this. I was known to have been quite the whizz at Pong and Frogger back in the day.

But no matter how hard, or how many times I tried, I just couldn't get past the first stage. I didn't even see who shot me, and I must have played and replayed that stage twenty-five times. Each time I would shuffle carefully up to the corner of the building I was trying to infiltrate. I would peep around it and, instantly, the world went red and blurry, and the cut scene showed my virtual corpse slumped on the floor. With disgust I turned it off. I had some packing to do.

On arriving in the United States, I had put my old riding gear in storage in the slightly scary and vermin filled basement that came with the house we had bought. It was scary in the nature of all American basements. Dark and musty, and next to all of the rattling boiler and air conditioning equipment. It was vermin riddled because no matter how many times I sprayed for ants and cockroaches they always came back, scuttling into dark corners and crawl spaces whenever I was forced to venture down there, like some unwitting participant in a horror movie who hears that inevitable bump in the dead of night and decides the most prudent course of action is to go explore alone.

I found all of my gear where I had left it, somewhat carefully folded into one of the leftover packing cartons. I had sold my very expensive one-piece Dainese racing leathers when we left the UK for almost next to nothing.

But I had brought with me a black Gore-Tex armoured jacket that sported orange dayglo stripes down the front and back, and I still had my trusty blue Arai motorcycle helmet, a pair of leather gloves and some rather snazzy, bright blue, Frank Thomas armoured riding boots that would have looked the part had Kajagoogoo still been in the hit parade.

Everything was thickly covered in a layer of dust, and the blue Arai and its visor were coated with a strange sticky substance. I gave everything a good shake, expecting cockroaches to swarm out and make me hop around the basement in terror, but all was well.

I took all the gear upstairs and scrubbed and polished until all was restored to its former glory. At least I had some decent gear for the trip, even though I lacked a set of decent waterproofs. I figured I would be fine.

I looked at the map on the wall of my office. Suddenly the United States seemed to have grown significantly in size. Atlanta seemed very far south, somewhere near the tropics, and Fargo seemed to have shifted northwards to rub shoulders with the Arctic Circle. If I was to complete this trip, I figured I would need to plan contingencies for potential encounters with both Manatee and Moose.

I seriously considered buying or renting a GPS system for the bike. But in the end, it felt like being a traitor to my true self. No, I decided. I would complete this trip in the same way that I had completed all of the ones from my much more innocent youth, almost forty years ago. I would do it with an astounding level of foolishness and naivety, or not at all. I would leave whatever common sense I still retained behind. I would refuse to become mired in meticulous planning and unnecessary gadgets. I had Fargo as my end goal and a handful of what I considered to be interesting places and fun things to do along the way. The rest would be left to the Gods of providence and fortune.

I would complete this trip as I always had done. On a strange and probably unsuitable motorcycle, with the wrong and incomplete kit, navigating by paper maps like a pirate on the high seas. Travelling on a whim, a prayer, and like Blanche in a Streetcar Named Desire, on a reliance on the kindness of strangers.

I ordered a set of Rand McNally Road maps from Amazon that would cover the states I would need to ride through, and when they arrived my worried mind relaxed a little. The navigation looked simple enough. Compared to the United Kingdom anyway, where there are more motorways, A-roads, B-roads, C-roads, tracks, paths and unadopted byways per capita than almost anywhere else in the world, each one criss-crossing the other in an infinite matrix of confusion.

In the USA, in this vast but relatively young country, the available opportunities to get hopelessly lost were reassuringly few. I would need to use Interstates now and again, usually to avoid major cities, but the state roads would, more or less, take me where I needed to go without too much fuss or needless diversion.

While I was planning, packing, and panicking, the landline phone rang which it almost never did. The caller ID was unfamiliar, but it turned out be a Great Lakes number. It was Ben. Our hearts raced as we picked up and then clustered, ears cocked, around the hissing, static filled receiver.

He was only allowed a thirty second phone call. He told us that he had arrived safely at the Great Lakes Recruit Training Command and that he was doing OK. He sounded very small and far away, like an echo of himself from his childhood. From a time when he still needed me to be his dad.

His voice was stretched too thin, both by the long wires of separation, and the alien world he had willingly stepped inside of. We had so many questions to ask. Were you well? What was bootcamp like? Where were you sleeping? Did you get to fire a cannon yet?

But time had already ticked away. We could hear a training officer shouting in the background of the echo filled corridor we pictured him in, and the voices of other recruits queuing behind Ben to make their one phone call home.

"Gotta go. Bye mom, bye dad." He squeezed into his last second.

The click of the disconnection was deafening.

We wouldn't hear from him again for nine long weeks.

Off With A Wobble

Finally, all of the planning for the trip was complete. The weeks had flown by, and while we hadn't received another phone call from Ben, we had written a few letters to him and had received two or three in reply. It seemed bizarre to be communicating by handwritten letters. I felt like Mister Darcy as I sat at my desk struggling to remember how to form the letters with the unfamiliar Bic biro held in a cramping hand as I wrote — '*gadzooks young nave, by my troth, I do resolve to ink my quill and send a missive of good cheer across the many miles that doth sunder us.*' or something of the like.

All of my gear was packed inside a small set of throwover panniers I had borrowed from a friend, and a tiny tank bag that displayed my maps through its clear pocket that I could easily view while riding. I hadn't packed much. I figured on a maximum of four days to reach Great Lakes in Illinois and then another four to get to Fargo, allowing time for a few stops along the way. I could have completed the whole trip much quicker, but the whole point of the ride was that I wanted to see a few weird and wonderful things on the journey.

In my youth I would have taken a much too small tent, and a sleeping bag that already smelt like spoiled milk and camped along the way. Nowadays, being longer in the tooth and the owner of joints that creak and pop alarmingly when I do the least energetic thing, like sitting in, or getting up from a lowish chair, I considered anything less than three-star accommodation to actually be camping.

Rather than camp, I had decided to embrace living life on a dull knife edge of discomfort and frugality and stop only in cheap motels I found by the roadside. I would avoid the bigger hotel chains and try to find the good old fashioned, family run, mom and pop style motels that used to be so popular in the 1950s but have now been overrun, and almost driven out of existence, by the ubiquitous Holiday Inns and Marriott's.

Outside the house, standing in the baking heat and soaking humidity of the day, the bike stood waiting for me. It lurked like a threat. In my neighbours garage the Ducati had looked small and lean, easy to ride and comfortable. Parked at the top of my long drive the bike loomed like a thug outside a nightclub, it seemed big and heavy and suddenly I was filled with doubts. The shining black and silver bike seemed to crack its tattooed knuckles and bellow, in a Mister T stylee, "Whatchoo looking at! You can't ride ME old man!"

A big part of me suddenly agreed with it.

But Paula was watching me, and I didn't want to let her know how concerned I was that perhaps, riding motorcycles might no longer be my bag. I ignored the thousand butterflies that had decided to take spontaneous flight and the tongue that cleaved to the roof of a suddenly parched mouth and walked confidently over to the bike with a weak smile on my pallid face.

I threw a leg that had long since lost its flexibility and feel for a motorcycle over the unfamiliar bike. The 800cc V-Twin Scrambler felt low, the riding position was upright and relaxed. That was good. The last Ducati I had owned and ridden, a 996S, had given me the shambling gait of Quasimodo, forearms meatier than Popeye's, and fingers and knuckles more knotted and twisted than a plaited loaf.

I pulled in what I felt eighty-percent certain was the clutch and turned the ignition with a trembling hand. As the modern TFT display went through its sophisticated little start up sequence, I suddenly recalled with a jolt that I hadn't seriously ridden a bike in close to fifteen years.

I ran the controls through a mind filled with doubts. Could I actually still ride? With the clutch still engaged I cogged it down with my left foot. The bike made a satisfactory clunk, and the LCD display reassuringly informed me that I had selected first gear. I wasn't even sure how many gears this bike had, but they all seemed to be in the right sequence so far. I gave the throttle a hearty blip. The bike throbbed like a familiar Ducati V-Twin, and I felt a little more reassured.

I looked up to see that Paula was watching me with a face filled with the sort of concern a mother has for her toddler, stood waiting at the gates of the kindergarten, on the child's first day at school. I lifted the visor and blew her a kiss.

"See you in Chicago in four days sweetie."

"Are you sure you know what you are doing?" She asked, looking at me with a hint of side-eye.

"Oh yeah," I blustered with a cool nodding tilt of the helmet, "like riding a bike babe, you never really forget."

And with that little piece of bravado, I slipped the clutch, blipped the throttle, and, like a pre-schooler's first attempt at riding a bicycle without stabilisers, came to a jolted, jerking, awkward, and embarrassing halt as I stalled the bike. I nearly dropped the Ducati and simultaneously pulled a small but critical muscle in my back at the same time.

The first twenty miles or so were a challenge. My biking muscles, both physical and mental hadn't been fully stretched and exercised in the longest of times.

I think as a biker you never lose the instincts that scan each junction ahead for a car whose driver might not be paying attention, or checking for fumes from the exhaust of an idling car that might suddenly pull out into traffic. The constant scanning of the tarmac ahead for the location and potential slipperiness of manhole covers and slick painted white lines, but still, I was decidedly rusty.

The racing line I described around the first large roundabout I encountered was less smooth arcing circle, and more bumbling dodecahedron as I slipped the clutch, crunched the gears and bunny hopped my way around it in a series of semi-straight lines punctuated by wobbly, and uncertain sudden leans to the left and sporadic lurches forwards.

But the little Ducati was easy to ride. The bike had a low centre of gravity and it more than compensated for my tentative throttle inputs and slightly clumsy gear changes around unconfident corners. The seating position held me up into the wind, just the slightest of pressure on old wrists, but I was very comfortable as I rode west over the bridge across the south end of Lake Allatoona, the sun high in the sky.

It was hot. Holy shit, it was hot. My riding jacket was bought and equipped for a UK summer. One designed for wetness, chilly winds, and endless disappointment. As I rode west, I could still feel the ninety-five-degree heat of the day being reflected back up at me from the steaming blacktop. My race boots were claggy with moisture and my hands damp with sweat. I cracked the visor only to be pelted with small flies and the heated blast from a big trucks exhaust.

Only ever having driven in the United States, I had somehow conveniently forgotten that air conditioning was not an optional extra on a motorcycle.

The small muscle in my back, the one I had wrenched on my initial, failed launch sequence, was complaining, and I shifted restlessly around on the little Scrambler trying to find my place of ease on the bike. The miles drifted by. I passed Marietta and coasted slowly across country to pick up state road 78. This road would carry me west, parallel to the much faster and busier interstate road of I-20. But I was in no hurry. My plan for today was to meet up with an old English friend just outside the town of Talladega, close to the city of Birmingham Alabama.

Talladega is the home of NASCAR, and I had tickets for the race for the following day in my back pocket.

The sky above me was a perfect arcing curve of azure perfection. Not a cloud stood in the sky. Not a single contrail streaked to spoil natures creation. The road was mostly straight. In the very distance it disappeared into a fierce heat shimmer that rose from the baking black of the tarmac. Dust lay by the side of the road and on either side small lakes stood, flat and placid in deep meadows of wildflowers and drought stunted trees.

The small towns I rode through were typical of the rural south. Filled with the usual mix of Denny's, McDonalds, EZ Car Towing companies, and Dollar Generals. In every town I rode through was a white-pillared Baptist church always sandwiched incongruously between the local pawn broker and the gun store.

I still felt tight on the bike. I was concentrating too hard. Over thinking every braking manoeuvre and every gear change. The Ducati was forgiving of too high or too low a gear, but I was seriously making its life overly hard and difficult for what we were doing, which was essentially riding down a dead straight road with almost no other traffic to negotiate. I tried hard to relax my grip and let my feet dangle on the pegs.

The road was dual carriageway in both directions until I passed through the town of Tallapoosa. The road became a single ribbon of tarmac. Rural farmsteads were dotted across the wooded hills. Suddenly, I knew I wasn't in Kansas — well Georgia, anymore.

I passed a sign that read, "Welcome to Sweet Home Alabama," and the song of the same name accompanied by the familiar jangling guitar riff began to play unbidden in my head.

A movement caught my attention and I looked across to see three buck deer running across the field to my right. The muscles on their haunches rippled dark chocolate brown against their coffee dappled pelts as they bounded with ease across the meadow. Their pale flecked ears stood high, constantly twisting in my direction, and then flicking forward. Dark beaded eyes reflected the glimmering sunshine.

I watched them carefully. They were easily keeping pace with me, and I was afraid that they might seek to cross the narrow road and take me out in a puff of fur and a clatter of limbs, hooves, and wing mirrors as they did so, but instead they veered right and disappeared with a white tail flash into the woods.

I smiled to myself and realised that I had finally subconsciously relaxed on the bike. My body was still. Arms slightly bent, helmet pushed into the oncoming airstream, hands resting, not gripping the bars. Not a single thought or worry in my empty head. Just the twanging guitar refrain and Lynyrd Skynyrd's lyrics going around and around and around.

I guess old Neil Young hadn't been too complimentary about Alabama, in the song he penned and named for the state, what with his references to banjos playing through broken windows and old folks with white ropes. Certainly, the lyrics of Sweet Home Alabama give back as good as they get in regard to Mr. Young's thoughts on the state. But I could not deny that the countryside was breath-taking. Vast glittering lakes, handsome rolling hills bordered by towering verdant trees lay in every direction.

But it *is* also undeniable that the state has had a chequered part to play in history. Its politics have always been both deeply red and sometimes darkly religious. In 1861 Alabama inevitably seceded the union and joined the confederacy. Very few skirmishes occurred during the civil war on Alabama territory, but all through the 20th century, Alabama has continued to be a battleground state for racial discrimination, disenfranchisement, and segregation cases against its large, coloured population.

It even had a supreme court chief justice; one Roy Moore, install a statue of the ten commandments inside the capitol building in Montgomery. It was finally removed to much furore from both the religious right and those pesky lefty liberals in 2003.

The sun reflected off the tarmac. In the distance, the road disappeared into a tunnel of trees that grew close by the road. I was forced to squint against the glare and began to rue leaving my shades in the glove compartment of my Subaru back home.

The day was getting old, and I was getting a blinding headache when I finally took a side road just south of Oxford. As I rode into the town of Munford, I started to look for the motel we had booked for the night. It was a Motel 5 1/2. It should have been a Motel 6 but had recently been downgraded for reasons that would soon become clear. All the decent local accommodation had already been booked by the crowds flocking into the area for the race.

Adrian was already there, waiting for me in the room we were to share. The look on his face as I pulled into the car park told me everything I needed to know about the impending quality and luxury of our stay. If he had sucked a lemon and shoved knitting needles up his nostrils, he couldn't have looked more sour.

Sure enough, the carpet of our ground floor room fairly scuttled with activity and the taps rattled and coughed before emitting a burping 'shart' of rusty water. The brown ring around the toilet basin matched the shade of the soiled seat perfectly. The shit stains on the bog complimented the delicate hues of the curtains and the duvet. It all smelled as though an incontinent tramp had just been kicked to death and his body stuffed into the closet.

The stains on the floor of the closet indicated to me that it had most likely been a very recent killing, so I decided to keep my stuff stored safely in my panniers and tank bag balanced high on a rickety chair.

Without a word being spoken we exchanged a look and locked the door and walked down the dusty, desperately hot road in search of food, and any other pleasant distraction that might keep us away from the terrible murder room until the moment we were forced to return for sleep.

We found a packed place called Big Daddy's Bar-B-Q only a few hundred yards down the track that ran out of town. The restaurant was housed in a timber shack. The building had the appearance of something I might have hurriedly crafted from a pail of bent nails and some driftwood. But the smell of the food made my mouth drip like a St. Bernard sucking a chop.

There was not a whole lot else going on in Munford. Other than Big Daddy's Bar-B-Q there were three or four churches of various denominations, the building that was masquerading as our motel, and a fire department building.

We had to wait a few minutes for a table. We were forced to stand, half in and half out of the door to catch the waft of air conditioning. My back was baked to ninety-five degrees and dripped with the humidity of the setting sun and the other side of me was a cool and chilly sixty-five.

On the open grill the flames rose to sear and char great slabs of ribs. At the counter the chef was slicing briskets, the juices flowing onto the chopping board. The jukebox blared and the customers raised their voices in competition with both the music and each other to be heard.

We finally got seated in the window, on a small table with a cheap and stained plastic red and white chequered tablecloth. I ordered the buffalo wings, and a half rack of ribs and Adrian did the same. We ordered a pitcher of beer to wash it all down. Adrian was very excited about the NASCAR race. He was the sole reason we were here. I enjoyed MOTO GP and British Superbikes. I had even been known to doze through a Formula One race every now and again.

But Adrian enjoyed anything that involved an engine thrusting wheels and a human participant around a track. And I mean *anything*. He had been to GPs, BSBs, WSBs, stockcar, rallycross, drag racing, carting, hill climbing and motocross. The one event he had not witnessed was NASCAR.

We swigged the beer and ordered another pitcher. Tomorrow, Adrian would tick that box. I looked around the room through booze bleared eyes. There was a surprising amount of bib overalls on display all topped by red baseball caps, but everybody was friendly and intent on having a good time. Country music blared from the jukebox. Somebody called Webb Pierce wailed out the lyrics to, *"How come your dog don't bite nobody but me?"* and the crowd in the bar sang along loudly and joyfully.

My fingers were sticky with buffalo and BBQ sauce and my head tingled with cheap domestic beer. I was in bliss. America, and with her, Americans, can sometimes prove themselves to be the best of the best.

Another pitcher was ordered. And I believe at least one more. Perhaps two.

The next thing I was certain of was that somebody who could only be Big Daddy himself was flashing the house lights, and everybody was standing to leave. Unfortunately, it was then that I realised that I hadn't stood for several hours, and the copious beers had rendered Adrian and I into the human equivalent of two large, supermarket bags filled with soup. Two bags of soup that somebody had precariously balanced on two astoundingly tall wooden bar stools.

We helped each other down and made our way, on very wobbly and uncertain legs out into the warm and humid night air. Thunder rumbled in the distance, lightning outlined the distant clouds, and the meadows on either side danced with the thousand twinkling lights of the lightning bugs. Two bull frogs called to each other, sounding all the world like they were shouting "*Jug-O-Rummm, Jug-O-Rummm.*"

It really wasn't very far to get back to the Motel, but after twenty minutes of stumbling across sidewalks and almost being lost down storm drains on limbs that seemed to have been filleted, I seriously began to doubt we would ever make it. I thought I might have to call for an Uber to take us the last thirty yards, when a battered old pickup truck stopped in a cloud of roadside dust. A very attractive blonde lady, a veritable Daisy Duke, leaned out of the driver's windows and drawled, "Doo y'all boys neeyud enny hep?"

"I beg your pardon?" I managed to slur.

"Ahhh sed, doo y'all boys neeyud enny hep?"

"Oooh, that would be smashing. Lovely." I answered.

"Aw mayuh sweet lawd, y'all boys are Englisssh, ain't yah? "Whale, hup oun n'back."

It wasn't easy but with some leverage and skinned knees and knuckles we managed to drag each other onto the bed of the pickup.

"Whurr tew boys?"

"The Motel please," I answered.

"Wich un?"

"That un," I said. "I mean, that one," said while pointing at the low building only thirty short yards away.

Our good Samaritan gave me a look of utter disdain, drove the very short distance, and locked the wheels of the little Ford to generate as much road dust as was possible in the car park of the Motel 6. We sat for three or four seconds in the back of the truck, choking and rubbing the grit from our eyes. The last thing, we heard, as we climbed with significant difficulty from the bed of the truck, was our samaritan muttering something about Jesus in particular, and Englishmen in general.

Talladega

I woke up in the queen bed with a banging head. Adrian and I had slept together like Morecombe and Wise, or Bert and Ernie. The previous night was a distant blur. I got out of bed to put the coffee maker on. The gurgling, steaming, hissing sound woke Adrian and, blinking against the brilliance of the morning, we sipped our coffees in silence, seated on creaky white plastic chairs on the little deck outside our room.

There was little traffic on the road outside the Motel but we both knew that the Talladega NASCAR Geico 500 race was the pinnacle of the season, and the raceway was bound to be busy. We also had pit lane passes that we had to use well in advance of when the race itself took place, so we made one more recovery coffee and then packed up our stuff.

With throbbing heads and bleary eyes, and with a few wobbles, now having the additional challenge of a pillion to take care of, I re-joined I-20 and headed west. Traffic was still fairly light. I saw a sign for the Eastaboga Baptist Church and five miles later, one for the speedway. I pulled off the highway and joined a short queue of cars that were looped around Speedway Boulevard looking for spaces in the plentiful parking lots.

These are at least two things that America does brilliantly that immediately came to mind. Parking, and sporting events. In particular, parking at sporting events.

I once took the wife and kids to watch Liverpool play an evening footy match at Anfield in the UK. We drove twenty miles and when we arrived, we couldn't find a place to park anywhere. All the side streets had been blocked off and all of the municipal parking had already been taken.

By the time we found a spot, we had to walk so far back, in the pissing rain, it would have been easier to have just the left the car at home and hiked the twenty bloody miles from the house. When we got to the stadium, the footy was pretty good but it was just that. A simple, straightforward football match. No bells and only one whistle.

On the walk out of the stadium and back through the rain-slicked streets of Liverpool we were greeted with a heavy press of mounted police and the mental menace of potential violence from the lingering crowd.

The USA puts on spectacular sporting events. You can use the word spectacular because that is precisely what they are — they are spectacles. Very often, mostly at baseball games, it is easy to forget that there is actually a game underway. It is so easy to be distracted by the kiss cam, the tool race, the hotdogs, the beer and candy floss sellers, the dancing mascots, and the cheerleaders.

When we first arrived in the United States of America, my wife and I would quietly mock the Americans around us who stood, a hand pressed to heart, to sing the national anthem.

But the patriotism and the single bloody-minded belief that the USA is the best country in the world is beguiling. It is insidious. It creeps up on you and slowly captures your heart. It happens even if you never fully relinquish your sense of, deep down, being British. British, and altogether too fond of a nice cup of tea and a "mustn't grumble," attitude as you tread in more dog shit, and the rain begins to come down, yet again, on your carefully planned outdoor barbeque.

But it snuck up on us, this blatant, much too loud, far too confident Americanism. Before I knew what I was doing, I was chatting to strangers in boarding queues at the airport, asking for assistance at the hardware store and actually complaining to the waiter about the 'doneness' of my steak.

It wasn't very long before we became citizens, and we too stood proudly to the national anthem, singing along, a tear at the corner of an eye as the crowd honoured a returning and injured veteran. And as the final words, "*O'er the land of the free and the home of the brave*," rang out, loud and clear around the stadium, three F-15s screamed overhead to the cheers of the crowd that now included us.

I carefully parked and locked the Scrambler close to the gates. A security guard who bore more than a passing resemblance to Muhammad Ali promised to look after it for me. We showed our tickets, and we were inside. We were very early, so we decided to get a cold and frothy recovery beer and go for a long walk around the facility to get our bearings. We had a walk over to where our seats were located high in the OV Hill North Tower stands. From there we could see the entire 2.66 miles of the circuit and the infamous thirty-three-degree banked track.

We had to use our pit passes by eleven in the morning to allow the teams to prepare for the race, so we walked down and crossed the wide ribbon of rubber-streaked racetrack that separated the stands from the pits, to wander, blasted in the heat of the day, around the centre of the raceway where the teams were frantically preparing the race cars.

Milling all about us was the entire cross section of NASCAR patronage. I have to admit, on reflection, that the cross section appeared to be quite narrow and the gene pool shockingly shallow. The crowd was composed mainly of young white males who clearly disliked all things dentistry, but strongly favoured a mullet.

Three almost identical looking young chaps were stood in front of us as we watched the mechanics prepare Danica Patrick's car. They were short and lean, dressed identically in stained wife beater t-shirts and torn wrangler jeans. Each sported a moustache of the wispy and sparse variety that would have evoked my dear old Mum to remark, "I'll just wet me hankie and wipe that off for you."

They drawled in an accent so thick and slow that the meaning of the words eluded my ability to interpret. They appeared to have shared not only a hairstyle from the 1970s but also a single, snaggle tooth. It occurred to me that murders must be hell to solve in parts of Alabama, what with there being so little variation in the DNA and almost no dental records.

Adrian was known to be quite the wit himself, so when he saw our new friends, I could see the comedic cogs immediately starting to whirr and a witty phrase strained to loudly escape his lips.

I touched his arm. "Leave it Ade," I warned.

These three might be small and scrawny, but I was pretty sure they would also kick our arses without a moment's hesitation. They had the wiry build of rodeo riders and walked with the air of folks who didn't entirely give a rat's ass if the Sheriff himself was thereabouts.

"Come, look at the big, shiny brum brums," I said to distract him. We walked around the pits for a while, kicked a big pile of massive racing slicks that were piled up, and peered into the austere and thoroughly functional, reinforced cages in which the racers would shortly tear around the circuit in excess of two-hundred miles per hour.

While we still could, we wandered around the circuit to where the banked track reached its most extreme incline. It was almost impossible to climb the forty-five feet to the top so sheer was the slope. Like Sherpa Tensing and Edmund Hillary, together we slipped and staggered up the slope. At one point Adrian lost a shoe and nearly fell like a tumbling boulder all the way to the bottom but I managed to grab the back of his shirt to save him, like a good sherpa would. Just before we had to break out the crampons and the extra oxygen, we reached the top rail and peeped over the top to look out over rural Alabama, the steeple of a hundred Baptist churches, the only buildings visible through the carpet of trees.

It was even harder to get back down. We had to adopt the embarrassing old man bum shuffle. Just as we reached the safety of level ground a whistle blew, and the Marshalls signalled that it was time for the public to vacate the raceway.

It was desperately hot out on the tarmac anyway, so we journeyed back to the shade of the hospitality area. We drank another beer and enjoyed a hot dog or two. The general air of the pre-race event was reminiscent of a carnival. Jugglers entertained; the sponsors held raffles where you could win a ride-along in one of the cars. There was heavily branded merchandise to buy everywhere, team shirts, pennants, and models of the cars. Food was munched and beers were quaffed. Slowly the crows thinned, and we realized it was time to take our seats.

In the stands, we were exposed to a sun that blazed relentlessly, high overhead. The sky was clear and offered no respite from the pounding heat of the day. The crowd was at capacity. We were shoehorned into seats shoulders touching each other and those of our neighbours. My t-shirt was quickly soaked through and sweat dripped slowly down my back to dampen buttocks that were perched on the hard, plastic chair.

It seemed to take an age to get all of the forty cars onto the raceway. The pace car led the long snaking procession around and around the circuit. The stands were filled by splashes of team colours. The largest American flag I had ever seen pierced the azure sky at the end of the straight-away. The cars burbled past us again and again, and the stand surged with noise and excitement as the pace car finally pulled into the pits, a green flag was waved, and the race began.

The sound of NASCAR has been likened to rolling thunder, and as the race cars floored their engines as they swept by us to commence lap one, I fully understood why. The drivers formed up, sometimes two and sometimes three cars abreast as they continued to accelerate and work up, through the gears to reach top speed. It was thrilling. For precisely two laps.

At the start of lap three I leaned across to Adrian to ask, "how many laps are there in a NASCAR race."

"Close to two hundred." He replied.

"I — what the who now? Two *hundred*?"

"Yeah. It's a five hundred event. It says so on the tickets. Didn't you see that?"

"Yeah, but so what? Five hundred is just a fancy name isn't it."

Adrian laughed. "No mate. That's five hundred miles they race. Get comfy, we're going to be here for quite a while."

And we were. The drivers all had names like Bubba, Chuck, Curtis, Cotton and Buck. And not having a single clue who any of them were, we decided to support the only female driver of the same car that we had peeked into in the pit lane. That car belonged to Danica Patrick, and she was at, or close to the front for much of the race. I will spare you the blow-by-blow thrills of the next two and a half hours of my hot, sweating, tedious life.

It seemed to be only Adrian and myself who became quickly bored by the proceedings. The rest of the crowd cheered without pause as the cars swept by, again and again, and again, and again.

There were a couple of crashes and spin outs but nothing too exciting if I am being honest. More frustratingly, every time a car blew up or crashed into the banked Armco, the safety car came out and whoever had been leading would instantly be jockeyed out of position and fall back through the field.

This happened. A lot. Each time I saw the safety car I would glance at my watch and despair as precious minutes were added to the race.

The crowd loved it all. They literally lapped it up, lap after tedious lap. But of course, for them they understood the personalities. NASCAR is akin to professional wrestling. And just like professional wrestling, there are good guys and bad guys in NASCAR. There are feuds, fights, quarrels, and back stories, all constantly played out between the drivers and their teams, all acted out in ear shattering action and at over two-hundred miles per hour in front of them.

There was noisy blow by blow commentary blaring constantly from the one hundred speakers dotted around the circuit, and each time a car spun out, the crowd would stand and either whoop and holler or groan and throw baseball caps to the ground in dismay.

With only a few laps to go, and with my bum as numb as a lip full of novocaine, Danica Patrick finally took the lead. She was driving with incredible flair and precision, and I admit a small flutter of excitement that the horse I had picked, so to speak, might indeed prove to be the winner.

Unfortunately, some driver called Dick Trickle Jr the third, or something similar, crashed into the top of the banked track and spun out. With only a single lap to go, the race was stopped, the pace car came out and when the race was restarted, Danica was swamped by the pack and ended up all the way back in eighth place as the lead car took the chequered flag and victory.

As we walked out of the circuit and back to the bike, we both agreed on two things. The first thing is that whatever you want to say about NASCAR, it is NOT a race. Nothing like it in fact. I am happy for the fans to adore it and rave about the spectacle, but it is far from being a competition that can be won on skill, determination, or engineering excellence. And the second thing we both agreed on was that, for the remainder of our limited time on this planet, we would never agree to watch another one.

Muscle Shoals

I dropped Adrian off at the airport that lay just northeast of Birmingham. The one in Alabama, not the one with the traffic jams of Spaghetti Junction, the Bullring and the brummie accents. It was only a short but hot and humid twenty-minute ride from the raceway. It had been good to see him, but I was keen to get back on the road. There is something about riding solo that invigorates the soul and it had been many, many years since I had had the chance to savour that unsteady mix of loneliness and self-satisfaction that comes with it.

With both the bike, and my mood, suitably lightened I peeled out of the airport approach roads and took the dual carriageway directly north towards Decatur.

Traffic was busy on the outskirts of Alabama's capital city, and I got stuck behind a long, slow queue of two lanes of cars. In the UK I would have cogged it down and ridden slowly and safely between the cars. In the USA this is called lane splitting and, in most states, it is illegal. But then, so is riding blindfolded or wearing only socks on a motorcycle according to the statutes in the state.

On the contrary it *is* legal to run a red light on a motorcycle, although this is only allowed if the mass of the bike is too small to trigger the automatic sensors. It is also legal for bikers to ride their machines the wrong way down one-way streets. But you do need to have a lighted lantern with you, so that makes sense.

Helmet laws also vary wildly from state to state. Most states require helmets to be worn for those under eighteen, and only seventeen of the other fifty states require a helmet to be worn by riders at all times regardless of age. Only Iowa, Illinois and New Hampshire have no helmet laws whatsoever, so you can go there to feel the wind in your hair and then grind your dome down to the bone until you leave a long line of that somewhat useful squishy grey stuff on the road.

I turned off the freeway and onto the less used highway 31 and found myself in almost perfect isolation. The well surfaced road undulated between the low hills. Fast sweeping bends took me through a pleasant horse country. Large white painted antebellum homesteads stood like sentinels at the end of long driveways. I couldn't help but think, that at least some of these plantations would have produced cotton a century ago. The oak beams of their tile roofs creaked beneath the gravity of the import of all of the human misery and cruelty of that not so very distant era.

The afternoon was waning, although the heat of the day continued to plague me. At the dusty intersection of Highway 31 and State Road 67, I topped the little Ducati off with gas at the Kroger gas station, had a pee in the spotless bathrooms of the store and, back outside, emptied a frost topped bottle of water down my throat in one series of satisfying glugs. The dust from the road painted sweat stains down my face and neck and I popped back inside to buy two more ice cold bottles. One to drink and the other to pour, head bent between knees, all over my overheated neck and shoulders. The shock of the cold made me shudder and emit a small high-pitched squeak of shock and ecstasy that made a passing mother and daughter giggle unexpectedly.

I suppose that I was quite the sight. This man baby, clothed in a bulging riding jacket that would have fitted perfectly twelve years in the past. Sweating and red cheeked, water streaming down his face, and gasping for a breath against the desperate humidity of this sunny day that shone without end.

Back on the bike I turned onto state road 67 and then realized I had turned too early. I was intent on navigating with paper maps in the same manner in which I had ridden across much of Europe and Scandinavia when I was much, much younger. It turns out that I was not only younger back then, but also much more competent at reading maps on the go having not relied on Tom Tom, and Google Maps for the last twenty-three years.

My eyesight was also not what it used to be. I pulled over in a place called Gibbs Junk Yard, and with a rottweiler the size and ferocity of Cerberus baying for my blood at the thankfully locked and sturdy gate, I screwed up my eyes to squint at the tiny, blurred letters on the map inside the tank bag's transparent cover.

I was in luck. No need to turn back. I could still skirt the busy town of Decatur and get back on track by picking up Highway 72 just south of the Tennessee river.

The day was beginning to draw long. I found myself increasingly hunched over the tank bag. The relentless heat of the day had drained me, and I began to sporadically glance down at the map in front of me to see if I was getting any closer to my goal, the town of Muscle Shoals.

As I glanced back up to check that a juggernaut hadn't pulled out in front of me and that I wasn't going to end up spreadeagled on the back of the truck like Wile E Coyote running into a bogus tunnel painted on a mountainside by a malicious Roadrunner, I had my breath snatched away to see a hot air balloon rise silently above the tree line in front of me. It was a timely reminder of why I was heading all the way out here. I was going to take a ride in a hot air balloon.

I swept through a town so small that it seemed nobody could be bothered to take the time to name it. It could have been any town, anywhere, USA. It appeared that its sole reason to be, was to house the largest Lowes, Walmart and Home Depot stores I had ever seen. Dotted in between, and all around them, were the American staples of every rural community. An AT&T store, a U-Haul rental centre, A Big Lots, a Dollar General, a Zaxbys, a Cracker Barrel, a Captain D's and, of course, at least five or six MacDonalds.

It is a repetition that can be seen all over America. Powerlines stretched across the horizon. Huge traffic lights swung lazily above the broad and busy intersections. Vast steel sails of billboards towered into the sky, advertising space for injury lawyers and services to quickly obtain cash for structured settlements and annuities. Litter was piled in the gutters and poor people walked to their minimum wage jobs, parasols or simple newspapers covering their heads from the latent ferocity of the day.

I shook my head in frustration. Alabama and all of its southern neighbours have a rich heritage and enjoy magnificent countryside, but this unremitting regurgitation of urban decay has been allowed to infiltrate and take over the poorer communities.

And then to prove that I was at least somewhat on point, I crossed a spur of the Tennessee River on a long bridge and the scenery was transformed into a glittering panorama of flat peaceful water, bordered in the hazy distance by low mounds of tree covered hills that encircled a magnificent marble fronted country club designed to look like Camelot. Private yachts scudded across the ripples and far out across the water I could see the glint of a perfectly white speedboat towing a skier.

Surely, there must be a middle ground somewhere, poised delicately between these two seemingly opposed worlds.

Only a short ride remained of my day. I was meeting somebody in the church car park of Muscle Shoals at seven that evening. Time was ticking by, and I was beginning to think that I might not make it.

Finally, I pulled into the car park of the St. Luke Methodist Church on Avalon Street and parked the wildly pinging and dinging Ducati in the deep shade of some towering, purple crepe myrtles to cool.

Curt was waiting for me, stood by the empty trailer of his Dodge Durango. It was Curt I had booked to take me for a ride in his hot air balloon along the Tennessee River to see the sun set across this iconic piece of water and I was very excited.

I don't like to judge a book by a cover, but I suspected that Curt might be a big fan of NASCAR. He had a farmer's tan under his wife beater t-shirt and camouflage cargo shorts. His accent was as thick and heavy as a barrel of tar. He drawled a greeting and flashed a goofy grin as he walked over, and I truly believed that I might have been in the presence of one of the Gump family.

We shook hands, but I had to wince and look away in quiet English disgust as he hawked a bubble of chewing tobacco into the corner of his mouth and spat into the dust at his feet.

I took my tank bag and panniers off the Ducati and stowed them in the back of Curt's car. In the back seat I exchanged my riding jacket and jeans for some shorts and a t-shirt, and then off we went. The trailer was empty because Curt had left the balloon with his helper to prepare it for the flight. When we arrived at the empty field where we were to take off from, I was introduced to a surly, rake thin lad of perhaps sixteen. He never made eye contact or spoke.

"Dontcha nevermind bout Bubba," whispered Curt quite loudly enough for the boy to hear, "he be near half a bubble off plumb. He plenny strong though."

I have to admit that voluntarily jumping into a car with Curt and being driven to an entirely empty field in the middle of nowhere to meet Bubba had, so far, looked like a mistake of monumental proportions.

But the balloon, that stood dead centre of the green field, was impressive. It swayed slightly in the crosswind from the river, fifty feet across and sixty feet high, its bright red and yellow ripstop nylon was stretched taut. Fully inflated, it heaved at its moorings, desperate for the sky.

There was very little pomp or circumstance. I expected a little safety briefing, a plastic hard hat, a parachute. Something. Anything. But Curt just hopped over the side and summoned me to do the same. I levered myself over the edge of the basket and as soon as my feet hit the floor, the ropes that tethered us were dropped and the balloon rose, eerily quietly into the clear evening sky.

It was a motion I had not experienced before. Curt fired the burners once or twice and the roar was deafening just as the heat radiated down to make me wince against the burn of the flame, but otherwise, it was like floating. It had that dream like quality where you simply lose contact with the ground. Not flying, simply rising into the sky. We cleared the tree line and began to drift at precisely the speed of breeze, eastward down the river.

The wide ribbon of the river reflected the last rays of the sun back towards us. Far below I could see the splash of white waters as it broke and tumbled over the shoals that gave the town below its name. All was peace. Except for the dogs. Wherever the balloon went we were accompanied by the barking of every single neighbourhood dog. I can assure you that in stark disagreement to what Ed says in the movie 'Shaun of the Dead,' — dogs surely can look up. Every single dog in Alabama was looking into the sky and barking till it was hoarse, at the big scary balloon thing that sailed soundlessly above them. It was like somebody had let a cat loose in Battersea dog's home.

I had to raise my voice against the cacophony from below. "Tell me again, what was the name of the town where we met?" I asked Curt.

"Muscle Shoals."

"Why is that so familiar to me?'

"You heard a Lynyrd Skynyrd right? Sweet Home Alabama? The town is named in the lyrics."

I tilted my head. It *was* vaguely familiar. Curt continued, but this time singing. If it were possible, he sang in a flatter monotone than my own, but his southern accent and the tempo of the song made it unmistakable.

"*Now Muscle Shoals has got the Swampers,*

And they've been known to pick a song or two (yes, they do),

Lord, they get me off so much,

They pick me up when I'm feelin' blue, now, how 'bout you?"

I tod Curt that I had known that to be the lyric but hadn't thought that Muscle Shoals might refer to a town. This town. I asked him what a '*Swamper*' might be, and he explained that in the 1960s and 1970s, Muscle Shoals was known as the hit recording capital of the world. Everybody from Aretha Franklin, George Michael, Doctor Hook, Bob Dylan and the Rolling Stones, all recorded their music at the FAME studios on Alabama Avenue, right there in town. And Lynyrd Skynyrd too of course.

The Swampers was the local name given to the Muscle Shoals Rhythm Section. Artists were drawn to travel all the way to Muscle Shoals specifically to record with the Swampers because of the unique sound they had created. It was a southern mix of R&B, soul, and country. Altogether the Swampers put their music onto over seventy-five gold and platinum hits.

Paul Simon wanted to record with the Swampers, but when he asked for them, he found, to his dismay, that they never travelled. Artists had to travel to them, all the way to Muscle Shoals, to this very sleepy little backwater.

While we had chatted, we had both been a little distracted and had not noticed that the balloon was a little of course and had lost a significant amount of altitude. We may have been off course but what we were on course for was a collision with a tall Black Oak that stood proud on the banks of the fast-flowing river.

Before he did anything else, Curt took the time to drawl, "weeeell shiiiiit," and to spit out another brown blob of baccy before firing the burners in one long burning roar that only sought to intensify the pitch of the barking dogs below us.

The balloon desperately, slowly sought to rise. But the heat of the day was against any swift alteration in altitude. The bottom of the basket scraped through the uppermost branches of the tree and tilted us at a quite extreme angle for a few seconds. The friction slowed the balloon and suddenly, free of the grasp of the tree, we were dropping.

Curt fired the burners again, one long, deafening roar that, for a second, drowned out the noise of all of the barking dogs. I could feel the heat on my upturned face.

"Best grabba holda summat, fi were you," he mumbled slowly.

Suddenly, all of the calmness and serenity of the balloon flight was lost in a tumbled plummet into a bumpy, field, filled with poison ivy.

We were lucky. The balloon landed mostly upright and other than landing heavily on my arse cheeks in the bottom of the basket I was fine.

"Sorry about that," muttered Curt, "it c'n happen sumtimes."

Across the field I could see Bubba waving to us. He had followed us in the Durango, criss-crossing side streets, always keeping us in view, or possibly just following the sound of the dogs.

All around us poison ivy swarmed. I looked down at my bare legs and fervently wished I had kept at least my riding boots on.

Luckily Bubba had managed to open the gate at the top of the field and had backed the Durango and the trailer right up to the basket and the quickly cooling and collapsing balloon.

Late evening had turned slowly into early night and the first of the stars had begun to appear as the sun gave up its final glow on the horizon and the skies above had darkened to a deep purple. I helped a little with the loading of the basket, but Curt and Bubba had the packing of the balloon down to a fine art and I suspected that anything I contributed was likely to just slow them down.

On the way back to the church parking lot, Curt pulled into a CVS store and bought a packet of wipes that could remove the urushiol oil that poison ivy contains in its leaves, and which makes it such a nasty and persistent irritant. I don't think I had got any on me, but I wiped my ankles and hands with the wipes regardless.

Back at the bike I quickly pulled on my jeans back over the shorts and jacket over the t-shirt and waved goodbye to Curt and Bubba. I was exhausted. I had planned on riding north for a few more miles but just couldn't be arsed. I was also supposed to be on a budget but remembered that I had seen a Hampton Inn on the way into town so gave in.

I started up the Scrambler and rode the three or four minutes to park up in the back of the hotel's parking lot, beneath a building courtesy light and in direct view of a security camera. I walked wearily into reception, bringing with me all of the dust, the bugs, and the heat of the day into the gleaming, sterile, but refreshingly cool marble lobby of the hotel, much to the chagrin of the hotel manager, who stared aghast at the little trail of debris I left in my wake.

Civil War

In the morning I woke slowly and, with the intent on maximising my investment in the fancy hotel room, I showered using all of the soap and conditioner sachets, stole the shower cap, even though I no longer sport a single hair on my head, made three cups of sugary coffee, and then went down to the buffet to eat breakfast and to fill my helmet with bread, cheese and ham for lunch.

I felt much better after the solid night's sleep and, thankfully, there was still no sign of any redness or itching, so either I hadn't touched any poison ivy, or the wet wipes had done what they had promised.

I took the opportunity to call home. It was good news. Ben had phoned and confirmed that he had passed the Battle Stations simulation which is a key gate that the sailor recruits need to pass toward the end of week seven of their bootcamp process. If the recruits pass, they are allowed one more brief phone call home before the graduation itself takes place.

Battle Stations is a twelve-hour long simulation on an almost true to scale mock-up of a real Navy warship, the USS Trayer, a two-hundred-foot-long mock-up of an Arleigh Burke-class destroyer, all enclosed within a 90,000-gallon pool in a 157,000-square-foot building. The Navy trainers use Hollywood-style special effects to create challenging and realistic training scenarios.

The recruits get the chance to put into practice all the practical and theoretical knowledge and skills they have learned during the preceding seven weeks. The exercise includes firefighting, swimming, water survival, shipboard damage control and teamwork all set in a high-stress environment.

One of the most feared exercises for the cadets is to individually enter a smoke-filled compartment in full firefighting gear, wearing oxygen masks, and then to remove the mask. Thick, acrid smoke chokes the compartment, blinding lights pulse irregularly, blending with a relentless and unnerving soundtrack of a ship in distress. The sensory overload raises the tension and confusion brought on by a long night of physical exertion and mental stress, diminishing the recruits' visibility and confidence in equal measure.

It is an arduous twelve-hour test of confidence, knowledge, and stamina but Ben had passed. He was now officially a Navy Sailor and the Pass-In-Review ceremony in Great Lakes was on.

Back outside in the rising heat of the day, I checked the chain tension and tyre pressures while I secured the panniers and tank bag. The sky, as always, was clear blue, marred only by the turkey vultures circling on the thermals. Black dots under the palm that roofed my eyes. I got the distinct feeling that they had sensed fear and weakness emanating from the bald head far below and were intent on following their prey until he fell.

I was destined for Kentucky, but I had a few stops planned. The first of them was to the FAME studios on Alabama Avenue, Curt had told me about. I rode through deserted suburban streets for a few miles and then all the way down Alabama Avenue until the road petered out into a fishing dock that hung lazily out over the wide expanse of the Mississippi River. The Mississippi was broad and fast flowing, and the river level was exactly as high as the riverbank. It was unsettling to the senses to have something so large and immensely powerful just slip by mere inches from your toes.

I had a quick look around but couldn't locate the recording studio of such repute anywhere. The only person around was an was an old chap seated on a short and rickety looking deck that jutted out like a disgruntled chin above the water. He held an old fishing rod out into the fast-flowing water like a divining rod. The fisherman was thin, but the dock still looked barely able to support his weight. I didn't want to shout in case I disturbed the fish, but the last thing I wanted to do was add my weight to the dock in case it sent us both into the river to end up like two bobbing corks in the Mississippi delta four-hundred miles to the south of us.

In the end I tiptoed out to where he was seated, listening to the creak and pop of the board under my cringing toes. Through the wide cracks in the boards of the dock, I could see the green river racing beneath me. The movement was disorienting, like being on a ship in a heaving sea and I found myself suddenly unsteady, but I made it across to the old man safely.

The fisherman's name was Cornelius. His skin was the colour of obsidian, but he had crinkled laughter lines around both his eyes and mouth. He gave me a broad and mostly toothless grin to add another to his brow as he told me that the recording studios had moved years ago, and I needed to ride back into town where I would surely find it on Avalon Avenue.

I thanked Cornelius and fairly sprinted back to the safety of land.

On Avalon Avenue I found the recording studio, but it was closed. The building was modern, and utilitarian brown located between a CVS and a Pizza Hut. It could have been a hair salon or a place selling motor parts, so I got back on the bike with a sigh and set off on my way.

I guess it was good to know that I could still get excited enough to go ride to a random place based only on a stranger's side remark.

I started the morning by riding back the way I had come the previous evening. When I got to Decatur, I turned left to head north, crossing the Mississippi for the first time on the Steamboat Bill Memorial Bridge. I would cross the Mississippi many times on this long ride north to Fargo.

The Ducati was riding beautifully. I loved the thump of the v-twin and the comfort of the almost upright riding position. It was great to be back on a bike again. Just the open road ahead. The tranquillity of solitude. Riding to adventure and discovery. I had missed this. Too many years of being confined by the working week. Endless drives to airports, to fly into mostly pointless meetings in faraway cities, and then to fly back home, or onwards to the same, or similar meetings in another city in another state.

State after state, city after city I had travelled on business, and not seen much of this magnificent country other than one more unfamiliar airport, the inside of an Uber and yet another corporate hotel room, each one an identical facsimile of the last.

This trip would be different in every respect. The open road, a half-assed plan in my back pocket and myself, making the same stupid, ill-informed, and the frequently bad decisions I was famous for nearly forty years ago.

The road in front of me was a tangled ribbon of discovery, a fast lane to places both heard of and yet to be stumbled upon. This trip was a self-indulgency. I knew that. The Ducati a free bonus, and I intended to make the most of the slow, long ride up towards Fargo and the end of my trip.

The sun rose in the sky as the miles and the towns slipped by. Brownsboro. Gurley. Paint Rock. At Scottsboro I crossed the Guntersville Lake on the Veteran's Drive Bridge and crossed back into Georgia close to Trenton.

I cut across country on GA-136, taking the switchback roads to circumnavigate Cloudland Canyon State Park. It was cooler in the trees and my confidence with the Scrambler was increasing with every sweeping mile. But my little diversion, while it made me grin, also took me the very long way around.

It was early afternoon when I pulled up to the seemingly deserted stop sign that marked the junction with GA-341. I made sure to make a complete stop. The counties around here made good tax dollars from unsuspecting motorists, who in the middle of nowhere, and with not another vehicle on the road, slide through a stop sign. And sure enough, when I glanced down the road, a police cruiser was parked, almost completely hidden behind a giant flowering rhododendron bush.

I nodded to the officer, but I couldn't see through the glare of his windscreen if he acknowledged me, so I made a careful left turn to head back north towards Chickamauga. I was hot and drenched in sweat once more. My head throbbed from the stifling humidity.

It was with scant relief that I rode the Ducati into the parking lot of the Chickamauga & Chattanooga National Military Park. I had seen the signs for the historic monument from the road and despite having lived in the deep south of the United States for fifteen years, I had somehow remained blissfully, and quite possibly, wilfully ignorant of the events of the American Civil War. I thought it was time that I at least paid some attention to the war that so divided that still young nation, and to some extent, still does.

I parked the bike and bought an ice-cold Coca-Cola from a vending machine by the visitor's centre and, rolling the cold can across my throbbing brow, went back outside for a wander.

To be honest, I didn't really know what I was looking at. The military park spans 5,200 acres of meadows and trees, and the informational plaques, while very informative, are wildly spread out across that vast space. I saw some stands in the woods, and across the rolling fields, and another stand facing it. Piles of cannonballs lay scattered across the vista. I am not without imagination, but I just couldn't picture how a Civil War era battle might be fought in such a place.

I was thinking about heading back to the visitor's centre when I spotted an old guy stood by one of the plaques. He was engrossed in reading it, absentmindedly scratching his head as he did so and occasionally looking up and shaking his head in wonder. I walked across and peeped around his shoulder so that I could see what was holding his attention.

We got to chatting. Generally speaking, it is hard not to get to chatting with an American. For the bigger part they are a friendly and open bunch of people. Mostly happy to share their time with an inquisitive stranger and eager to help out one with a need.

My new friend's name was Dave. I guess he was just entering his mid to late seventies. In a past life, he had been a marine and as predicted, he was both friendly, chatty, and luckily for me a full out civil war afficionado.

Dave touched me on the shoulder to turn me around to face the battlefield. His face lit up as he started to describe the action, and the battlefield in front of me began to come, slowly, to life. Dave pointed at a clearing.

"See that? That's Elijah Kelly's farmstead. That's where the first engagement took place. Thomas's union soldiers stumbled quite by accident on a battalion of confederate cavalry. The first shots were fired, and the battle was joined."

He told me how Brigadier General William Rosecrans had believed the confederate army, under the control of Braxton Bragg, were in rout. Rosecrans had pursued them, from the city of Chattanooga, south and into Georgia. Unfortunately, for Rosecrans, Bragg actually had most of his reserve troops stationed in the town of LaFayette not far from where we now stood.

Dave told me how the lines had moved, pointing to the barricades in the woods, waving his arm to explain how the cavalry charges had advanced and been decimated by musket and cannon fire. For three long days the two armies had attacked and defended, penetrated, and repulsed. Now I could begin, at least a little, to see through Dave's eyes. To see what he saw.

Thousands of troops, dehydrated in that summer's drought and the dreadful heat of a Georgia day, marching through the rising dust. Building desperate defences from hastily felled timber from which to defend the relentless to and fro of the attacks. Loading and discharging black powder weapons, the blinding smoke rolling across the bare meadows where the bodies of both men and horses began to pile.

The screams of the wounded, the shouts of the generals, the endless detonation of cannon. The ring of sabre on sword, the thunder of hooves

In the end, the key to confederate victory was a mistake by Rosecrans. He believed a gap had opened in his flank. He ordered Brigadier General Thomas Wood's division to fill it. But no such gap existed, and Wood's advance only proved to create a division wide hole in the Union position, where previously there had been none. The confederate army took immediate advantage and advanced in three lines.

Dave and I walked slowly across the field to where the rout would have taken place. We puffed and panted our way up a steep hill and looked back down on the battleground.

"This is Horseshoe Ridge," said Dave. He seemed emotional. His eyes were red and watery as if he almost remembered the scene that had played out that last evening all those years ago.

"This is where Major General George Thomas made a last stand for the union. They called him '*The Rock of Chickamauga*,' after that. He held the confederate lines back until darkness fell and the last survivors were able to escape, back north to regroup. In total, 34,000 men, on both sides, both union and confederate died on those three days. The tragedy is that every one of them was an American." Dave told me.

We shook hands and departed. Dave had parked his car at the back side of the hill on which we stood. I walked back across the scene of the battlefield on my own. Thanks to Dave's brief but passionate education, I now found myself re-imagining what it must have been like.

The civil war was fought for nearly exactly four years and, while it seemed to me to be something that happened in very distant history, it was surprisingly close to the modern era. Only a few generations separated the lives of the soldiers from their modern-day descendants. War was declared in April 1861 and peace declared in April

1865. That's a scant one-hundred years before I was born. The American Civil War resulted in the deaths of 620,000 men. Almost two percent of the population of the USA at that time.

I guess, to a degree, that helps explain why animosity still festers in parts of the south, and the occasional confederate flag can still be seen flying outside rural homesteads in Georgia and neighbouring Alabama and Tennessee.

Back at the bike I discovered that the cost of entry to the visitor centre met my '*every penny is a prisoner*' criteria. So, with absolutely no entry fee required and the blast of air conditioning luring me inside, I decided to have a look around. Well, bugger me twice in one day. Magnificent. Inside is the usual diorama displays that American's in particular seem to love. Clumsy effigies of civil war soldiers, with dead button eyes and wax faces that always seem to have been held too close to a flame, all dressed in moth eaten tunics lined the displays.

But then I turned a corner and found myself in a room filled with corridor after corridor of handsome, polished glass fronted oak framed display cases. Inside the cases was one of the most impressive collections of weaponry I have ever seen.

Blunderbusses, flintlocks, bayonets, cutlasses, sabres, pepperboxes, wheellocks, muskets, musketoos, and carbines. There must have been a thousand weapons, all in pristine condition, each one carefully labelled and helpfully explained.

I read all about the Minié ball. Apparently, its invention, just prior to the Civil War breaking out was key to the devastation of lives and limbs that the American Civil War produced. Never before, in the history of human conflict had such a projectile been so devastating on the battlefield. Like the invention of the longbow or the cavalry charge, it changed how wars would be fought. Before the Minié ball, soldiers fired spherical lead shot from unrifled weapons. Round shot and unrifled weapons were both inaccurate and lacked range.

The Minié ball was conical and fired from a rifled barrel. Not only was it more accurate, the Minié ball had greater velocity and possessed greater range. On impact the cone of the Minié ball flattened, causing massive trauma to tissue, blood vessels and bone. Amputations were common and were often the only treatment available to field surgeons to avoid the spread of gangrene and subsequent death, in a time before the advent of germ theory and the discovery of antibiotics.

All that information and history, here in this innocuous little building located just outside the even more innocuous town of Chickamauga.

The confederates proved themselves victorious at Chickamauga, but my next stop on the bike was at Lookout Mountain just a few miles north. The battle there, a few months later, on the outskirts of the city of Chattanooga would fall in favour of the union and prove decisive. It gave the union control of the city known as the 'gateway to the deep south.'

At the conclusion of the battle, one confederate soldier was famously said to proclaim, that. "This…is the death-knell of the Confederacy." And so, it proved to be.

I was less impressed when I first crossed into Tennessee and pulled into the car park at Lookout Mountain. The site possessed breath-taking views out over the great loop of the Tennessee river that casts its watery arms around the city far below, but I didn't bump into Tennessee's version of Dave, and so didn't actually find the visitor centre or even the site of the battle.

It was all just too spread out between the trees for me to really appreciate, given the limited time I had to spend there. The only abiding question I was left with after navigating the almost sheer winding road to the summit was, how on earth did they get the bloody cannons up there?

The afternoon was starting to wane when I got back on the road. I was heading for a road I had been told about by a colleague soon after I arrived in the USA.

In England we have some pretty cool biker roads, or at least we used to have them. The Snake Pass, and The Cat and Fiddle were two of my favourites. They have now been thoroughly de-funned by having average speed cameras installed along all of the once thrilling, and occasionally, admittedly dangerous, twisty bits.

Not so the '*Tail of the Dragon,*' This is an eleven mile stretch of road that runs between North Carolina and Tennessee. It may be short, but for an American road it is conspicuously twisty. There are three-hundred and eighteen curves to negotiate in those eleven miles. The road is bordered by the Great Smoky Mountains and the Cherokee National Forest. The bends are tight and come thick and fast with very little run off for those who are heavy on the wrist and low on common sense.

The sun dappled the tarmac and blinked blindingly through the tall trees that flanked the ribbon of road. The little Ducati thrummed its steady beat and pulled with vigour down the longer stretches, the brakes leaching speed with ease to negotiate the twists and turns of the dragon.

Those long-forgotten biker senses had started tingling again, and as my confidence increased, I started to move my weight around the bike, flicking left, accelerating hard, scrubbing speed with just two fingers on the brake lever and a touch of the rear to stabilize the bike and then flicking right.

I was very conscious that I was rusty and riding somebody else's motorcycle, so I didn't push the envelope, and it was fortunate that I was taking it somewhat easy as just around the next bend a state police cruiser was parked, the handheld speed gun pointing in my direction.

The road runs through Blount County and the cops there are pretty hot on keeping the traffic on the Dragon firmly within the posted speed limits. There is a reason for this. In a ten-year period, this eleven-mile stretch saw twenty-seven fatal motorcycle wrecks — four more than on the rest of Blount County's eleven-hundred miles of road in the same time period.

If you do crash and survive, you can stop at Deal's Gap and add your recovered wreckage to the '*Tree of Shame*.' The tree is covered in the coloured parts from motorcycles that have crashed, or been '*bitten by The Dragon*,' at some point in time.

It bears a sign that reads "No gain & a lot of PAIN!"

And that's the other factor in play here. This is rural America. VERY rural America. If you crash on the Dragon, you best have a high pain threshold and a tourniquet handy because an ambulance is going to take over an hour to get to you, and with the nature of US health insurance it will immediately bankrupt you when it arrives.

When you think rural in the south, not only is a great deal of it remote you should also be thinking Dukes of Hazaard, Cletus, Cooter and Boss Hogg rural. The film Deliverance was filmed not far away in north-eastern Georgia, and there are reasons why stereotypes exist. Tourists can white-water past the famous rock where Burt Reynold stood, and by the side of the road, the locals sell shirts emblazoned with the slogan, "If you hear banjos, paddle faster."

The local supermarkets are predominantly Piggly Wiggly, and the front yard of each timber framed home is the owner of at least one broken down and rusting pickup truck. This is the part of America that smacks of moonshine, chewing tobacco, NASCAR and a bitter unwillingness to admit that the south truly ever lost.

I rode through the centre of Knoxville and crossed into Kentucky close to the rural town of Jellico. Jellico is the caricature of American small towns that British folks carry around in their heads.

Two storey rows of brick-built shops, housing ironmongers and barber's shops, haberdasheries and drug stores. Many windows boarded now, but still with signs of a lucrative past. The streets were lined with wide and sensibly angled parking bays jutting into the broad street. American flags were everywhere, hanging from offices, factories, civic buildings and homes. There is the obligatory Walmart and CVS of course. But also, a smattering of family run '*Mom and Pop*' type stores, hanging onto retail survival with every dime and cent spent in their now struggling communities. The only offices that seemed to still be doing great business were the gun stores, the pawn brokers and the office of '*Diddy, Cheateonher and Howe — Divorce Lawyers*'.

I rode as far north on highway 25 as I could, until I came to the town of Richmond. With the sun setting, and being too exhausted and hot to continue, I fuelled up the Scrambler at the Four Corners Market and Deli store. I bought myself some ice-cold Pabst Blue Riband beers because I wanted the taste of a cold beer but didn't want to get in any way drunk, and a sandwich the size of my head, and started to look for a motel for the night.

I found one eventually. All the signs for accommodation pointed towards the chains that surrounded the local airport, but I found what I was looking for in the Sunset Motel.

It was located on a four-lane highway in between a power sub-station and the Colonial Heights United Methodist Church. I parked the bike outside reception, creating a cloud of dust that hung in the air around me. I removed my helmet with some clammy difficulty and then poured out the sweat like I was emptying a fishbowl.

The heat still rose in waves of punishing heat, unabated from the tarmac at my feet, even as the last rays of the sun dipped behind the row of ugly, towering electrical pylons and gaudy billboards.

I looked across at the church. It was the typical new build of America. Red brick with white colonial pillars and a white topped steeple. I am not the greatest fan of churches and religion in general, but the sign out front made me smile broadly. As I wiped the sweat from my eyes and unzipped the zipper of my jacket I read, through eyes squinted against the shimmering heat haze:

'TOO HOT TO KEEP CHANGING THIS SIGN.
SIN BAD, JESUS GOOD
DETAILS INSIDE.'

The Sunset Motel

I guess I should have checked out Trip Advisor first, but by the time I had checked in and connected to the limited WiFi it was just too late. These were the first six reviews I read when I finally got connected.

"Bring shower shoes."

"It's a nice place to trap out of but I wouldn't want to live there."

"Nasty, never again."

"Can we say Crack alley?"

"It's needs to be remodeled or better yet just plain tore down."

"If you were looking for a 3rd world experience this place is for you."

"It is cheap."

And so, the Sunset Motel lived all the way down to the very lowest of my expectations. It was indeed cheap. And, as all of the other reviews I later pulled from Trip Advisor attest, the owners of the Sunset don't have to overly worry about competition from the nearby Hilton, Marriot, Hampton Inn, or even the Rosebud Motel from Schitt's Creek.

The motel also provided, without asking or additional charge, a little miniature zoo in each room, in the form of silverfish in the bathroom, bugs in the bed and cockroaches, *everywhere*.

But, as I say, it was cheap and so, bang on budget. I hung my damp jacket over a chair in faint hope that the asthmatic air conditioning would air it dry and cracked open what had once been a cold beer. The rattling refrigerator in the room seemed to have raised their temperature at least ten degrees.

I had a room on the first floor. Or second floor if you are an American. Not the ground floor anyway. I am starting to confuse myself now. My room was up precisely one flight of stairs. I sat outside on a white plastic chair and took in my surroundings.

The sun was just setting over the slaughterhouse and the smoke from the crematorium on the very edge of town lent a hazy romanticism to the scene. It was still hot but dressed now in shorts with bare toes splayed against the splintered timber decking, and a tepid, flat beer in one hand, it was at least bearable.

I spent a miserable night in the Sunset Motel. What with the antiquated and thoroughly emphysema riddled air conditioning unit that seemed intent on shaking itself into a rattly afterlife, and the shouted death threats and sounds of smashing glass from the room above me. The room on either side of mine seemed to be rented by the hour. All night long, at clearly paid for units of time, the door would slam, and the bed would creak pneumatically for six or seven minutes. Then a forty or fifty-minute-long silence. I don't know what the couple next door did during that quiet time. Dressed and played a little whist, or a hand of canasta perhaps, but during this pause in proceedings, I would slowly drift into a troubled sleep only to be woken with a start, when time was up, with another slamming of the door and a repetition of the panted, creaking cycle.

At four-thirty in the morning, I finally gave up on sleep. It was probably a good thing anyway. I wanted to hit the road before the sun truly rose in the sky to cook me once more, like an overly clad burrito on a griddle. I had a long ride ahead of me. I needed to be north of Chicago to pick up Paula from O'Hare, and then ride up to the much nicer hotel we had booked close to Great Lakes Naval Station so that we could see Ben at his Pass in Review graduation ceremony the following day.

The skinny guy who had been on reception the night before was still there. He had his cowboy boots on the desk and a Kentucky Wildcats baseball cap pulled over his eyes. He was leant back so far in his chair that I thought if I woke him with a start, he was sure to fall backwards and render himself unconscious. Although, judging by the state of the sheetrock behind him this may have been a regular occurrence.

I gave a little cough like any English gentlemen placed in such a situation might do. This elicited no response, so I called out. Softly at first and then louder until finally, he came to life, pulling the cap from his eyes and miraculously lowering his chair gracefully to the floor.

"How'k'na help y'all."

"You were good enough to check me in last night and to lock my Ducati in your garage. Can I get it out please?"

He yawned so widely, and for so long, that I thought he might suffer from a bout of hypoxia and fall to the floor at my feet. But when he finally finished, he just beckoned to me, "folla me."

We walked back through the office and into the car park behind the motel. Darkness still clung to the sky, blanketing the car park, and turning the treeline a midnight blue.

Rain had fallen gently through the night and the car park shone with the reflected light of the neon streetlights from the nearby interstate.

In the far corner of the car park was the little garage where my sleepy friend had been kind enough to offer to secure my bike away. He struggled with the lock for a few seconds but then levered the door up with a loud screech to give me entry. As I struggled into gloves and helmet and secured my tank bag and panniers, he enquired.

"Did y'all have a gud nahhht."

I thought back to the constant disturbance from the other rooms, the unsettling scuttling of the vermin, the damp carpet, moistened by who knew what combination of bodily fluids, and the all-pervading smell of relentless putrefaction. I was just thankful that I lacked a forensic blue light in my tank bag.

"It was lovely thanks," I smiled.

Sometimes, it can be really tough to be British.

I rolled the Ducati Scrambler out of the reeking garage, swung a leg over and while I watched my helpful reception worker walk back towards his desk, I pulled in the clutch and fired the bike into noisy life. I blipped the throttle as loudly as I was able and then piloted the Ducati around the back of the rooms, pausing every now and then to pull in the clutch and roll back the throttle, watching the digital bars of the tacho swing across to indicate the redline. The little Ducati burbled cheerfully and raucously.

"Yeah—you motherfuckers, y'all can all wake up too," I muttered to myself, and then turned back onto the highway and headed north.

Chicago lay six hours away. A mostly tedious charge through Kentucky and Indiana before reaching the southern shore of Lake Michigan and crossing into Illinois.

Today would be a day of Interstates. I didn't have the time to spare for interestingly twisty country or state roads. No hours to kill on divertingly pretty shortcuts and lengthy diversions. I wanted to avoid towns as much as possible and just eat some miles. I passed close to Lexington and then headed west to cross the Ohio River in Louisville before the sun fully rose into the sky and the roads filled with commuters.

The Ohio river was a dead calm. It shone like a vast sheet of burnished steel as I crossed the bridge. On the northern shore I left Kentucky and entered Indiana. I had crossed the Mason-Dixon line, leaving Dixieland behind me and the familiar warm embrace of the deep south.

The Mason Dixon line was named for the two English surveyors Charles Mason and Jeremiah Dixon, in the 1760s. The tale is a staple of American middle school education. I remember my two boys both bringing home heavy tomes that told exclusively of North American history, and absolutely nothing about the rest of the world outside her munificent borders.

Charles Mason and Jeremiah Dixon were sent by King George II to create a border that would settle a lengthy and ongoing land claim dispute between Pennsylvania and Maryland. The border that the two ultimately surveyed became synonymous as the division between the slave-holding states below the line and the free states above.

On my journey so far, the deep south of the United States, as always, had been a perpetual enigma to me. In many ways it is a friendly and unassuming place to bide awhile. The south prides itself on its hospitality. But many times — not always, but still, far too often — that shoe only fits if both the shade of the face and the sexuality of the newcomer meet its own narrow terms of acceptance.

It is a place defined by its searing heat and suffocating humidity. It is made conspicuous by its fireflies, magnolias, creeping kudzu and the sound of bullfrogs set against the rolling thunder of summer storms that can shake buildings. Its lands are the Okefenokee and the Blue Ridge Mountains. It is the ancestral home of the Cherokee, the Muscogee, the Seminole and the Timucua.

When we arrived in the United States it is where we had chosen to make our home, and we loved almost all things about it. But the deep south always carries with it the sheathed edge of a confederate sabre. There is an uncomfortably deep vein of religious zealotry running through its poorer and more disenfranchised communities, and casual racism bubbles constantly beneath its tranquil surface.

I let Louisville slowly disappear in my rear-view mirrors and drove north. I passed through Memphis and Austin, Vienna and Edinburgh. Not the more famed cities located in Tennessee, Texas, Austria and Scotland, of course, the cities I now passed through were all located firmly in Indiana.

The United States has an annoying, while perhaps understandable given its size, habit of naming towns and cities after pre-existing towns and cities. In the USA, there are ninety-one places called Washington for example. Forty-five Franklins and thirty-nine Clintons. In a nod to nostalgia and homesickness, many towns are named after the places from where the original immigrants originated. There are thirty-two Chester's, twenty-nine Bristol's, twenty-eight Dover's, and twenty-three Manchester's. These are a few tiny examples of what can cause you navigational conundrums as you ride across America.

Massachusetts and Connecticut are filled with familiar sounding towns such as Everton, Cornwall, Glastonbury, and even Leominster which is surely not pronounced in the same way that the English pronounce it. Brits say Lemster, Americans say Leo-minster. Which actually makes way more sense the American way now that I write it down.

Even my hometown of Southport has a distant cousin in North Carolina. I admit that the town in North Carolina is prettier, with a harbour, much better sandy beaches and a crystal blue sea that contains almost one hundred percent less sanitary towels and turds than the one I grew up paddling and freezing my infant knees in.

Wherever you come across a place name that sounds cool and original, you can pretty much bet that it was re-purposed from the original Native American names — Nebraska, Mexico, Dakota, and the names of the most southern states — Mississippi, Alabama, and Tennessee for instance, they were all based on regional Native American words for features such as settlements, rivers, lakes, and mountains.

As I had been pondering this, I noticed that the sky had darkened. To the west a bank of clouds was quickly rolling in to overtake me. I passed close to the town of LaFayette (thirty-six of these), when the first big raindrop hit my visor with a resounding whump and a splatter. And then the heavens opened. The rain came down like some gigantic cow was pissing on a flat rock and within seconds the interstate was a boiling ocean of bouncing raindrops.

I, of course, had failed to consider that on a journey of several days I might encounter the occasional hint of inclement weather, so had failed to bring with me any waterproofs.

The bike began to shimmy in the standing water. I was forced to roll off the throttle. The big trucks began to barrel past me, heaving what water that wasn't already in the air back in my general direction. A steady trickle of startlingly cold water was already making ingress at the back of my neck. It was making its way steadily down the rear of my jacket to pool in the crack where my Batman motifed underpants met the Ducati's seat. The visor was a streaming opaque bubble of racing water droplets. It was like riding through a watery version of a Windows 3.1 starfield screen saver.

I slowed and pulled up to park the bike beneath a broad overpass to just wait out the passing of the fast-moving storm. A few seconds later I heard the deep but familiar *'potato, potato, potato'* rumble of Harley Davidson motorcycles, and three riders pulled out of the torrential downpour to park up alongside me.

Somebody in a darkened and beer fumed bar late one night, once explained the strange engine noise that is so unique to Harley Davidsons. It is to do with the odd choice of 45-degree V-Twin engine layout the bikes original designers chose. Like today, at the time of design, the company was very strapped for cash. The company had just been rescued by a Bowling Ball manufacturing company of all things and funds were limited.

So, the engineers settled on a very simple design indeed. Both cylinders would be offset by a forty-five-degree angle and uncommonly share a single crankshaft. To make matters worse, or better, depending upon your willingness to forgive lazy design for the sake of a serendipitously famous bark, the designers didn't have the funds to figure out how to spark cylinder one and then to independently spark cylinder two, so they just sparked up both cylinders together regardless of where they were in the ignition sequence.

So, now, cylinder one goes 'Po'. Cylinder two goes 'Ta' and while the crank rotates the pistons all the long way back around in their very asymmetrical power stroke sequence, a spark plug needlessly detonates some unburnt gas back in cylinder two, making the 'To' sound.

The Harley riders were all guys about my age, but all a good foot and a half taller and with much better beards. I could see them smirking at my armoured and dayglo splashed riding jacket. They all wore fringed leather jackets, assless leather chaps and German soldier style open-faced helmets with flying goggles. They all rode tourers.

Now, let me first say that I have absolutely nothing against Harley Davidson, her splendid motorcycles or the wonderful folks who ride them. We are all bikers. All fair and square, riding and enjoying the same roads. But, as I glanced from my little Scrambler to these three enormous riding machines I had to question if the Ducati and the Harleys were even in the same genus, never mind species.

There was an Electra Glide, a Street Glide and a Lube Glide. I may be making that last one up. But each of the Harleys must have weighed 1400 pounds apiece, each one three times the weight of my little bike and all only making about the same horsepower.

I took a ride on a friend's Sportster in the early eighties and loathed the riding position and centre of gravity. These Glides looked ten times more top heavy, although I might have swapped for one of the sail like fairings for a while, based on the current weather situation.

We shook hands in the rainstorm and chatted about destinations. Two were called Mike and one was called Donald which I thought was very unusual for an American. I figured that he might have been the first new Donald I had met in the fifteen years since we moved to the USA.

I told them my plans. They were making their way slowly across to take part in the Sturgis motorcycle festival to be held in a few days in South Dakota. They looked and acted like Hells Angels, but it turned out they were all salesmen in the same high tech software company. Sturgis was the one week they escaped their wives and tame subdivision lives to all ride out together and play at being '*Wild Hogs.*'

As we chatted, the rain stopped, and a sliver of blue replaced the smudge of darkness on the horizon. I had a plane to meet, so we said our goodbyes. One of the Mike's swapped numbers with me and he told me, if I had time, to swing by to see them in Sturgis. I told them I would think about it, swung a leg over the Ducati and powered off to re-join the traffic on the slowly drying road.

The country I now rode through was flat and featureless. Distant towns hugged the skyline, rows of pylons marched across the landscape, like a scene from war of the worlds. I passed a sign that said Chicago – 109 miles and thought I better hustle if I was to get to O'Hare in time to meet my wife's flight, but it was hard to make speedy progress. The interstate was mostly just two lanes, and with not being able to lane split, I was often stuck for mile after mile behind two trucks, one passing the other at precisely point two of a mile per hour faster than the other.

I needed gas, so had to pull off the interstate and follow the signs into a small rural town called Egypt. Why the United States cannot do service stations like the rest of the world never ceases to amaze me. In pretty much all places in Europe, you can pull straight off the motorway into a safe, clean, well provisioned rest area and have a wee, fill up the bike, buy a sandwich and, if you are fortunate to find yourself in Holland, some marijuana, and then be happily on your way. The rest places in America mean you have to stop at least twice. Once for a pee and a coke, then pull back off the interstate to find a gas station and sometimes a third time to find a drug dealer.

The town of Egypt was composed of a creek, the gas station, a single farm, and a vast and splendid cemetery lined with row after row of elegant marble headstones. The cemetery disappeared over the distant horizon, the gleam of marble headstones reflecting back the sun behind me. Where they were finding a steady supply of corpses to bury was beyond me, because I didn't see a single soul.

After another ninety minutes of riding through the world's largest corn field, I finally started to see signs of urbanization. I passed a sign for Crown Point and then drove past a vast medical centre building and then — crash. I was back into the land of fifteen-minute oil change stations, taco outlets, drive through liquor stores and the row upon row of the ubiquitous golden arches.

The interstate took me north, almost all the way up to the edge of the lake, close to Lake Street Beach, and then swept me left and west into Illinois and the windy city of Chicago.

I checked the time and figured I could spare a few minutes to ride the shore road up and through the city centre, the blue vastness of Lake Michigan an almost constant and watery companion to my right.

Lake Michigan is technically a lake, I get that. But to somebody brought up in the UK, who measures lakes by the distance you can throw a crust to a duck and sometimes even reach the other side, and who was always taught that Windermere was enormous, Lake Michigan is a veritable ocean of freshwater. Its surface area measures a truly gargantuan 22,404 square miles. The entire country of Wales would fit comfortably inside its watery borders three times over. Over six hundred ships have been lost in its extensive, and often dangerously stormy depths. It is also home to the '*singing sands,*' which squeak when you walk on them due to the high quartz content of the white dunes.

I passed the Navy Pier, the high crowding high rise of downtown to my left. Families were out taking in the sunshine, riding the Ferris wheel, and eating ice cream, but I didn't have time to stop. I made a left turn onto Irving Park and passed close by the iconic Wrigley Field.

Twenty minutes later I pulled into the parking lot of O'Hare, locked the bike, and waddled as best I could in my awkward racing boots into arrivals to get a coffee and wait for my wife.

Pass In Review

Paula and I got dinner together at a Wild Wings restaurant close to the Naval Training facility and turned in for an early night. It was lovely to see Paula, even though we had only been apart a few days. We were both excited to see Ben graduate. Paula lay awake for a while, tossing and turning in the unfamiliar bed.

Lured into slumber by the lack of both scuttling vermin inside the pillow and the sound of gunshots in the room next to mine, I slipped into a sleep as deep as a coma in the comfortable bed at the Hampton Inn.

In the morning, we showered briskly and drank a quick coffee. I wasn't sure how long it would take to clear security at the gate of the Naval base. At the time we didn't hold US citizenship so expected a long delay while the security detail wondered why our passports didn't look anything like the ones they were used to seeing.

We left the Scrambler back at the hotel and took an Uber to the base. At the security checkpoint we only had to show driver's licenses and were waved through to follow the signs for the graduation ceremony. The driver dropped us off close to a pair of large white metal doors.

Great Lakes is colloquially and rather comically known as '*Great Mistakes*,' and is formed around one-thousand separate buildings. On arrival, the recruits are assigned to a '*ship*' which is really the equivalent of a command. There are seventeen ships, and they all have the types of names we associate with warships, The USS Constitution, The USS Triton and of course The USS Enterprize.

Ben had been assigned to ship seven, The USS Chicago.

We cleared another layer of security and had to pass handbags, and wallets through a metal detector and then walk in single file past an extremely chilled out looking Labrador who had red bloodshot eyes and a perennially hungry expression, probably from sniffing too much hash every day of his life. We all took seats in what appeared to be a tiered sports stadium and then the ceremony began.

The new sailors began to march into the hall and all of the parents craned necks to be the first to spot their son or daughter, dressed in their smart dress whites. A marching band led the way. Banners and flags were raised, and the officers and training staff took their positions.

The problem in spotting our child, was that the Navy had gone to great lengths to strip the cadets of any iota of individuality. All were terribly young, fresh of face, slim, and dressed identically, with similarly cropped hair and shaven faces. Everybody looked almost identical.

Then we saw him. Ben was doing his best to stay in step with his comrades and keep eyes front while he sent searching glances around the crowd to see if we had made the ceremony.

At the end of the fanfare, some special awards were made, and then all the anxious mums and dads were allowed to spill out of the tiered seating to hug and embrace and congratulate their respective offspring's. Ben gave us both a hug and we took some photos. We were allowed to leave base with him for up to four hours, so we decided to take him back to the hotel so that he could shower and use the bathroom without forty other grubby recruits watching and waiting, and then go get some lunch.

It was hot outside and as we walked back through the base Ben paused every time he passed an officer, standing to attention and saluting. It was all very strange. Ben had never shown any respect for authority. I thought at first that he was doing it as a bit of a joke and would soon chill out and take the piss out of the officer behind his back when we had put some distance between him and us. But no. Ben's face was always serious and always one hundred percent respectful.

We got another Uber back to the hotel. Ben was in the hotel bathroom for the longest time. He had always been the kid who had no personal shame and will quite happily dig a hole in the woods and camp down with a bunch of friends in the wild, but I guess that eight weeks of doing your business in stalls with no doors and a drill sergeant shouting at you to "squat and drop," had been a dump too far, even for him.

Afterwards, we got some deep pan pizza at a joint just outside the gates and as we ate, I could see Ben glancing constantly at his watch. All through lunch he was quieter than normal, respectful, and contemplative.

We wanted to ask questions, to know what the CIA had done with the real Ben, and who this polite but strange Ben doppelganger was. After only an hour Ben's level of anxiety peaked and he asked us to take him back to base. He was worried sick he would miss muster even though the pizza place was only a very short ten-minute walk away from the gates of the base.

We finished the meal and I asked for the check, but it turned out that one of the locals had seen us with our new shiny sailor and has picked up the entire tab. I knew I should have ordered another couple of beers, a pudding, and three packets of fags.

We dropped Ben back at the base and gave him another hug. We wouldn't see him again for another six weeks. He was bound for Pensacola in Florida to attend 'A' school to learn the trade he had signed up for. In true military logic exercised the world over, he had had to pick a branch of the navy when he first arrived. Even though he would be a citizen when he left, he hadn't been one when he went in, so any job that carried the need for a security clearance was beyond his reach. He had chosen to work as an airframer, servicing military aircraft and helicopters. With all of the constraints, I thought he had made a good choice.

I know it's an age-old adage, a standard cliché, that the military will change you, but when we hugged and said our goodbyes, the transformation the Navy had performed on our somewhat wayward son had been stunning. Ben was a new person. Respectful, happy, and filled with the optimism of his new career.

What Paula and I had not realised, until this point, as we walked back towards the security gates, hand in hand, was that our future life with Ben would now, only ever be, could only ever be, a long series of farewells.

Des Moines

The next morning, I dropped Paula back at O'Hare for her Delta Airlines flight back to Atlanta. I had only a few days left before I had to meet the buyer of the Scrambler in Fargo, and I had a couple more places on my wish list to visit before I did so.

With Paula safely back at the departures terminal I navigated the bike around the endless airport loops and out onto I-294, south and then west on I-88.

I was heading for Iowa and its capital city — Des Moines. My reason for wanting to visit Des Moines was as piss poor and sketchy as the reason I wanted to visit most places in my life.

Des Moines had been the childhood home of Bill Bryson, the esteemed travel writer. I was a big fand and had devoured each and every one of his books. For some reason of flawed logic, I had always wanted to see the place of his childhood.

I took Interstate-88 as far as Aurora, just to facilitate clearing the city and the multitude of small towns that cluster like the dimples on an areola around the vast feeding nipple that is Chicago.

The towns there were clapboard and quaint, and unlike the area close to O'Hare, they were affluent and well-maintained, linked to the windy city by the '*L,*' the elevated train system that carries commuters on double decker trains quickly to jobs in the skyscrapers of downtown.

I left the interstate close to Prestbury and continued west on State Road 30. I thought the Romans were a dab hand at building a straight road, but they had nothing on a road construction crew from the Midwest.

I passed through many neat and small rural towns, Big Rock, Shabbona, and Union Grove. Tiny communities built amidst the endless rows of corn, pastel painted and pretty. South of Clinton I crossed the Mississippi on the Gateway Suspension Bridge and entered Iowa for the first time in my life. It looked remarkably, and somewhat depressingly like Illinois.

That of course is the problem with travel in a country as big as North America. Travel thirty miles in the United

Kingdom and you have crossed two counties, the countryside has changed from seaside to mountain, the name for bread rolls has changed at least three times and you can no longer understand a single soul.

In North America the landscape can stay the same for days, only Boston and Minneapolis have unique and easily differentiated accents, and Chick-Fill-A is everywhere.

I stopped for some coffee and a bite to eat in Mt. Vernon. I bought the coffee from a sweet little place called Fuel on the high street, and then parked the Scrambler under some shady elms close to the lake, in the local park, to eat the copious and entirely free lunch I had secreted in my helmet during breakfast at the Hampton Inn that morning.

The sun was high in the clear blue sky. I unfolded my map on a picnic table and did some calculations. I hadn't told Paula, but I really wanted to try and get to Sturgis. The problem was it was way off my planned route. Today was a Tuesday. I needed to be in Fargo by Thursday at the latest. If I stopped the night in Des Moines, as I had originally planned, I couldn't make the distance in the time that remained. But if I stopped in Des Moines only for a quick look around, and then ploughed on to spend the night in Sioux Falls, then I should be able to spend a night in Sturgis before heading north, and a long day's ride, to reach Fargo the following day.

I re-packed the bike, wiped the crumbs from my chin, and hit the road. To save some time I got back on the Interstate and let the throttle roll wide and open. The day was glorious and for a change a cool breeze swept in from the north. The miles flew by, the concrete ribbon of road pulled me through vast fields of golden corn. I was riding, fast and free, charging like a bareback rider on a painted pony through the tallgrass prairie of the North American Great Plains.

The roads were quiet and the horizon devoid of the usual signs of urbanization, just the occasional water tower or grain silo, hinting at the location of a distant farm or small town. The roads were dead straight, not a distracting turn or a bend to entertain. The bike burbled reassuringly beneath me.

It was fun for twenty minutes or so, and then I slowly realized that this pretty but monotonous landscape was not going to change anytime soon. If at all.

The scenery passed me by like one of those black and white movies from the 1930s and 40s, where the couple in the clearly studio-based car drive past the scenery that repeats itself every thirty seconds or so. Endless corn field, distant grain silo, small brown bird on a fence post. Endless corn field, distant grain silo, small brown bird on a fence post. Repeated, again, and again and again and again...

I yawned widely and began to wonder how I had made what should have been a fun little ride into such a marathon of mind-numbing monotony.

It was close to two in the afternoon when I finally reached Des Moines. I passed the Des Moines Register building where Bill Bryson's father worked as a sports commentator and journalist and then parked up the bike on 2nd Avenue, in a spot that overlooked the Des Moines River.

I had a little walk around but there didn't seem to be a real downtown to speak of. It was a little like Los Angeles in that respect, a mass of urbanization clustered around its grid of streets. It seemed to lack a centre. That definitive feature of a place. The Pike's Place of Seattle, the Fisherman's Wharf of San Francisco, the Acropolis of Athens, the Tower of Blackpool.

Des Moines was unremarkable in the extreme, the very dullest of all the rusty, dusty, dull blades in the kitchen draw. It was becoming clear, even to me, why Bryson had left and moved to the UK. I admit to being slow to an extreme degree. He had made it abundantly clear in his first book when he had written, "I come from Des Moines. Somebody had to."

As I often did, I pondered what was wrong with me. Why was my DNA so skewed to the peculiar and less visited. Why were all of my destination choices so left of centre. Honestly, tell me? What was really wrong with the bright lights and endless carefree distraction of a Las Vegas or an Atlantic City?

With time now at a premium I jumped back on the bike. With the revised plan in place, I had another four-hour ride, in a dead straight line, westward through the remainder of Iowa, before turning north and heading into South Dakota.

I will spare you the ordeal that was Iowa. The state motto of Iowa is, "*Our liberties we prize, and our rights we will maintain.*" It really should be, "*Flat as a plate of piss and nowt but corn.*"

My heart skipped a beat close to the ghost town of Loveland, a town so bereft of everything, that even Google Maps has passed it by. I had to make a sweeping right turn onto I-29. I had seen the signs for Sioux City for quite a while but still, the sudden bend took me quite by surprise after so many endless miles of not turning anything at all.

The change in direction made the blood pound in my veins with hope and anticipation of a change in the scenery. I found myself praying for a hill, or even a hump or a molehill. But the flatlands stretched on to a smoke hazed horizon in every direction.

I caught a distant glimpse of Nebraska across the Missouri River to my left and then the river ran close by, parallel to me as I rode through Sioux City. The city had a cool name but remained an enigma. Any view of it was masked by the vast railroad shunting yard and banks of elevated concrete. I almost called it a day when I saw a sign for a Motel, possibly cheaper even than the Sunset, but decided that I needed a change of scenery before allowing myself a pause in this journey.

I crossed into South Dakota just north of the invisible city and continued north, as straight as a Sioux arrow, continuing through the interminable prairie.

I finally pulled off the interstate and into the suburbs of Sioux Falls. At first blush it appeared that I had ridden all of this way only to find myself in a replica of Des Moines and I admit I despaired. I failed to find a tatty looking hotel that might meet my budget and, far too weary to continue, I finally acquiesced and parked the bike in an underground and secure car park that was in the possession of a Holiday Inn located on North Main Avenue.

I showered and lay on the bed naked, revelling in the blisteringly cold air conditioning for a good thirty minutes. I then changed into shorts and a t-shirt and walked into town to get a giant juicy rare steak and seventeen or eighteen beers to drown my sorrow and ease the soreness of my already rare arse cheeks.

After the disappointment of Des Moines, I didn't expect Sioux Falls to offer much at all but the downtown was a joy, and the water falls and shoals that excite and spume the gurgling, splashing water of the Big Sioux River, that runs directly though the centre of the town was a delight and a refreshment to senses dulled into defeat by the monotony of the days ride.

BADLANDS

In the morning, I awoke with a pounding head and an urgent need to decorate my toilet bowl. My arse was like the mouth of a bat filled cave at twilight. I must have had a bad pint. Or seven. While slowly recovering with a plain black coffee in one shaking hand, I texted one of the Mike's I had met when sheltering from the storm beneath the underpass near LaFayette to let them know that I was planning on a flying visit to Sturgis.

I didn't expect a response. I was certain that the Harley guys would have forgotten about the offer to meet up and show me around, but only thirty seconds later the phone dinged, and Mike texted me back with the name and address of a bar they frequented.

I had a five-hour ride across more Midwestern nothingness, so I packed my meagre and increasingly dishevelled looking belongings, and with knees pressed together to suppress accidental leakage from my suddenly unreliable bowels, I quickly visited the breakfast bar in the dining room, filled a helmet to brimming and then took the elevator down into the subterranean parking garage.

I emptied my helmet full of too sweet ham, tasteless American cheese, and sourdough bread into my little tank bag and, with a resigned sigh, pulled the helmet on, breadcrumbs falling into my eyes, and cinched up the chinstrap.

The road out of town led me close to the southern boundary of the Sioux Falls airport. A Delta passenger jet was on final approach. It roared overhead as I passed some golf club or other, and I was immediately homesick. I even thought about ditching the bike in the airport parking lot and just catching a flight home, back to Atlanta and my lovely wife. I could be there in less than three hours, sat in my own armchair, cuddling my dog Archie and sipping on a cup of Yorkshire tea, made unsatisfactorily tepid by our 110-volt American kettle.

But of course, I had a responsibility to deliver the Scrambler to its new and probably increasingly worried and impatient owner, so I turned north onto I-29 and then took the slip road west and rolled the throttle back to join I-90.

I guess I had been secretly hoping for a sudden change in scenery. A distant snow-capped mountain range or a twisting road through an ancient forest. But of course, the Midwest of America is uniquely mundane. It was dullness and tedium personified. Flatter than a Yorkshireman's cap, South Dakota stretched its monotony from one distant hazy horizon, without a single interruption or distracting feature, all the way to the other distant, even hazier horizon.

I don't believe I had ever been able to see so far in my life. In every other part of the world I had travelled, my view had always been interrupted by a building, a tree, or a geological lump in the ground. In the opposite way that the Inuit have a thousand words for snow I began to wonder if Midwesterner's had *any* words for the things that the rest of the world knows as lumps, hills, and mounds.

Around ten-thirty I had an unsettling and worryingly gurgle of the guts and fearing that if I inadvertently tried to release a little back pressure in the form of a fart, I might drown in brown in my jeans, I pulled off the road to find a public bathroom.

I found what I was looking for at the Aktá Lakota Museum & Cultural Centre just on the outskirts of Chamberlain, which is a sweet little town that is perched elegantly above a fetchingly satisfactory bend of the Missouri River.

I happily had what turned out to be just a pee and a reassuringly dry and sustained trump, so I had a quick look around the museum which is definitely worth a look if you are unfortunate enough to find yourself in the middle of literally fucking nowhere.

It was in the museum that I learned that the Dakotas were the ancestral home of the Teton Sioux.

For a good thirty minutes or so I read in awe of this tribal people's troubled history. Of course, I didn't know it at the time, but these very tribal leaders had informed and influenced a large part of my childhood. When I was between the ages of four and fourteen, I ran around various playgrounds pointing index and middle fingers at a feathered foe who insisted on circling my wagons for a reason a very young and naive me didn't at all understand.

This place in which I now stood was the actual land of Sitting Bull and Crazy Horse. The sudden realization made me a little dizzy and I had to find a chair to sit down in for a moment.

It was Crazy Horse who famously wiped-out Custer's troops at the Battle of the Little Bighorn in 1876. A year later, after almost continuous forays and hostilities, the tribal leaders, in a vain attempt at achieving peace, ceded some of the Black Hills territories to the ever duplicitous government of the United States.

But of course, that would never be the end of the conflict. Fourteen years later, Sitting Bull was killed at Standing Rock, and soon after, defeat for the native populations became sadly inevitable, with the killing of hundreds of native American men, women, and children at the hands of the US Cavalry, at what became known as the Wounded Knee Massacre.

Back outside I sat by the banks of the broad and shimmering Missouri River. I made a sandwich and contemplated the brutal taking of these tribal lands. There are still many Indian Reservations in this area, and the Black Hills territories are still contested, but this time arguments are confined, mostly, to the courtroom.

I was about to jump back on the bike and resign myself to my boring ride across this endless prairie when an informational sign caught my eye. Apparently, I was only a few miles north of the Badlands National Park. Now, all that I knew about the Badlands was that Bruce Springsteen had a song by the name, but my interest was piqued, and then the deal was done, when I saw a picture of the pale jagged peaks and rugged valleys of the area.

I looked at my watch. I had planned on drinking a late lunchtime beer or six with the Harley boys but, being this close, I figured I had time for a small diversion.

I pulled off I-90 at the Badlands Loop and headed south on State Road 240.

At first blush, this was the same flat, featureless terrain I had been riding through for days and then, to add insult to injury to this famously penny-pinching Englishman, I pulled up to a National Park barrier and was asked to pay $25 to enter. On my map the road had appeared to be a normal public road, so I was somewhat appalled to be halted by a barrier and a demand for a toll.

I seriously considered turning around. I craned my neck over the guard's shoulder to see if I could spy a craggy outlook or two, but the horizon beyond was unrelentingly flat and empty. The road infinitely straight.

"Is it really worth the twenty-five bucks?" I asked the guard.

"It's awesome bud."

"Hmmm," I muttered, rooting around in my tank bag for the correct notes.

I was still deeply sceptical. I love most Americans. I genuinely love their optimism and self-belief, their patriotism and confidence, all the things that most of my dour British brethren lack. But the word awesome is used for all sorts of circumstances that can be very far from inspiring awe. Anything from simply asking how somebody's day is going, to your enquiry about the root canal they just had.

The road that passed the Rangers station rose gently for a long boring mile or so to reach a high bluff and then I pulled into the car park located there with a long protracted, "fuuuuckk...meeee."

Like a magician pulling back a curtain, the Badlands were revealed in one sweeping and fractured vista. Like rows upon rows of incisor teeth, reaching in spectacularly replicated, sharply eroded buttes and jagged pinnacles, they stretched into the distance, made hazy by all of its vastness.

It was all very destabilizing. Here in this endless, featureless prairie was suddenly revealed a geological marvel, painted in startling, clearly defined strata of honey coloured iron deposits and icy grey silicas.

I rode through a twisted and tortured landscape on suddenly twisty mountain roads. Towers of stone reached into the sky, moulded by a millennium of driving wind and sweeping rains, carved by pure unrelenting, elemental nature, each one looking all the world like gigantic, towering termite mounds.

I was suddenly plunged into a world of elevation changes and hairpins. To my surprise, I easily transitioned from the boredom of the endless plains to one of seamlessly matching gears, trail braking and engine braking to the rapidly changing topography.

This land had been occupied by the Lakota people for thousands of years and the harsh but strangely accommodating geology made it easy to imagine them living here, making camps, sharpening arrowheads, making art, and skinning bison hides.

The wind whistled through my visor and the Ducati thumped, a Lakota pipe and bass drum, a Buffalo Skies prayer song to the nameless Gods of Animism — the Gods of the plains who controlled the lives of the Native American tribes for the eleven-thousand years before the white man came and destroyed all that seemed natural and understandable to them.

I swept around bends as smooth as Jimmy Carr's forehead, and gunned the little engine, a broad smile back on my face. I realised that I had bonded forever with this little Ducati. She was a joy to ride. She had played a reassuring part in the safe return of my riding nerves and muscles.

The scenery everywhere had indeed proved itself to be truly awesome. I still wasn't convinced it was worth twenty-five dollars, but the relief from the banality of the Midwest for a distracting hour or so had been most welcome.

At Pinnacles Outlook I headed back north and almost immediately, the magician stepped back onto the stage and swept his cloak across the vista to once more magically conceal the Badlands behind a sweeping green, tedium filled grassland.

It was close to five in the afternoon when I finally pulled into Sturgis. I was hot, exhausted and in a spectacularly bad mood which may have, at least partially, explained my next experience.

Half a million people attend one or more of the ten days of the Sturgis Motorcycle Rally, and it seemed that a quarter million of them were on First Street to greet me. Bikes stood in long rows, parked handlebar to handlebar for as far as the eye could see.

Chrome gleamed amid a veritable ocean of red, white, and blue. Girls in bikini tops strolled down the boardwalks giving out flyers that advertised bars and concerts. Crowds jostled, elbow to elbow. The constant rumble of Harleys was a steady background to the country music that blared from the bars, and the odour on the warm breeze was the scent of hot dogs, leather jackets, stale beer, skunk, and gasoline.

I rode carefully down the main road, looking for the Knuckle Saloon where Mike the Harley guy had said he and his friends would be.

Harley Davidson, the company, love this rally. They had a huge, sponsored banner stretched right across the main street proudly proclaiming in giant letters, "WELCOME RIDERS."

Little wonder. The bikes here were ninety-eight percent Harley Davidson. There were Sportsters, Low Riders, Fat Bobs, Street Bobs, Road Kings and a plethora of Glides, but there were also trikes and customized choppers, Bobbers, Baggers and Hardtails. I was beginning to feel a little out of place on my dusty little Italian Scrambler.

Even though the Sturgis rally is a free event, and not owned by any corporation, it still rather sinisterly manages to represent everything that the Harley Davidson's marketing brand department works extremely hard to evoke.

That evocation is freedom and the American dream. Bikers were here from all corners of the country and from nearly all states, although when questioned, many had shipped their bikes on trailers across the country to ride here. I even saw one bike with a sticker that read, "I rode my bike to the trailer rally."

In some ways the need to do that is somewhat understandable — the USA is genuinely enormous. I was already on day five of my ride and rapidly running low on both stamina and clean underwear.

I found a spot to park the Scrambler and walked into the Knuckle Saloon to get a cold beer and see if I could spot either of the Mike's or somebody who might be called Donald. It was tough. Everybody was at least twelve inches taller than me, and everybody was a Hells Angel or looked like they really, really wanted to be.

Hairy, tattooed arms stuck out of sleeveless leather jerkins. Chains hung from jean pockets. Heads were either completely shaved, or heads and shoulders were covered in mounds of greasy locks. There were a few guys there too.

I spotted the two Mike's and a Donald sat around a small table close to the bathrooms. I elbowed my way across and took a seat as we all shook hands once more. A waitress brought me a Miller Lite and I sat for a few minutes listening to the three guys talk shit while country music blared from the sound system.

The three were reminiscing as so many Americans do about the college experience, they had all shared. It is an almost uniquely American thing to do, and you can hear it everywhere you travel across the United States. There is an intense rivalry about college that is not only reserved for the so-called Ivy League schools. In Georgia you didn't really graduate if you didn't go to Georgia Tech despite there being several other schools of great repute in the area.

Baltimore has John Hopkins, Indiana has Notre Dame, Houston has Rice.

Every conversation about college life and how difficult the programs where, how tough life was and how expensive it was to finally graduate is a game of competitive one upmanship played out by adults who haven't walked a college quadrangle or thrown a mortar board into the air in the best part of thirty-something years.

The only worse thing in the USA than going to the wrong college is not going to college at all. It has started to go that way in the UK too to be fair. It used to be that leaving school and picking up a trade like electrician or plasterer, or an apprenticeship in engineering was the proven and honourable path to take. But no longer. Now you have to go to college to get a $30,000 dollar degree in ceramics or media studies and then work at Burger King for the rest of your life to pay it all back.

Neither of my two boys went to college, and all we heard from friends, colleagues and neighbours were commiserations on the same level as an unexpected death in the family or news that the new baby was born ginger.

I was bored shitless listening to the nonsense, so I jumped in and asked these '*Collegiate Hells Angels*' how the bikes had ridden since I last saw them, seeking to turn the conversation to something fresh.

Mike One turned out to be the worst type of braggadocios American male and I instantly took a strong dislike to him. I tend to do that anyway. My missus may have mentioned to me once or twice in our long marriage that I can be a touch on the judgemental side, even if she finally agrees that I have seldom subsequently been proven wrong.

Mike One launched into a long diatribe about the wisdom of choosing Harley Davidson and the obvious demerits and downright un-American and unpatriotic nature of choosing any alternative, which immediately prickled the hairs on the back of my neck, there being absolutely no hairs on my head left to prickle.

Mike Two, and even usually silent Donald, tried to jump into the conversation to steer Mike One away from his chosen course, but he was far too intent on education rather than conversation.

Mike One rambled on to extoll the virtues of Sturgis, an event purportedly independently organised and run, but which clearly carries only Harley Davidson's marketing message to the leather clad masses. Mike One even tried to explain to me, in minutia, about the supposed genius of Harley Davidson's marketing and product strategy. But I was already done. Eyes glazed by dullness and blinkered enthusiasm for only things built in America, I finished my tasteless, weak domestic beer and stood. I pretended to go for a piss, and just never returned.

Sturgis as an event *is* impressive. But culturally, the motorcycle scene that it represents is as far from what I consider, in my humble, if somewhat sarcastic and admittedly British and caustic sense of humour, motorcycling to be.

I grew up on meeting up with some mates on a damp, break-neck speed ride to Rivington Barn, or a crazy, semi-suicidal blast across the Snake Pass or the Cat and Fiddle, dicing with death on thin, slippery wheeled, four-cylinder Japanese bikes, equipped with only loose head bearings and a pair of red, aftermarket Marzocchi shock absorbers.

We all wore oil-stained jeans, white t-shirts, and leather jackets. We wore our hair long, until mine finally fell out with my scalp and decided to permanently leave we did anyway. We went to rock nights on a Saturday, we head-banged to Black Sabbath and did the '*wanking dog,*' to Status Quo.

Sure, we had a few Hells Angels in my hometown. The Satan's Salves were our local chapter and we feared them for good reason. But for most of us, the concept of an actual motorcycle gang was anathema. We were all just bikers, kindred spirits having a laugh, chasing birds, drinking pints of snakebite, and scraping pegs on Sunday afternoons on our over '*duraglit*' polished second-hand bikes.

Sturgis represents something uniquely American. The idea, the philosophy, of the Outlaw Motorcycle Club. And as Mike One had proven to me, there are thousands who have bought into the dream, the idea and, despite all evidence and facts to the contrary being readily available, they persist in their cognitive dissonance.

The concept of Sturgis really originated when the American veterans from World War II came home in the 1940s, and was further distilled by the returning, and largely unwanted veterans of the Vietnam war in the 1970s. Disenfranchised by society, they sought what they missed in the company of the like-minded. A fraternity of men who rejected societal norms, where the sense of brotherhood was reflected in the Hogs they rode, the tattoos they sported and the colours they wore.

Keen to reassure the public that not all motorcyclists were thugs and criminals, the rather clean living and mild-mannered American Motorcycling Association claimed that 99% of American motorcyclists were in-fact, law-abiding citizens like themselves.

In one single statement whose motive was intended to reassure, an entire culture, the 1% were born.

Almost coincidentally at the same time, a small and struggling motorcycle company's machines were featured in the film 'Easy Rider' starring Henry Fonda. The film plotted this emerging and exceedingly controversial culture. Easy Rider was a huge hit, and the legend of Harley Davidson was born.

Harley Davidson as a company is once more struggling financially. The reasons are simple. The Japanese and Italian motorcycle manufacturers are continually updating and reinventing both themselves and their machines. Who can honestly keep up with the current version of the Kawasaki ZX-R? Above all they know that to grow, or to even survive, they must market hard to create a new pool of riders and buyers for their products and expand their market reach across the globe.

When the United Kingdom brought in power restriction legislation for young and entry level riders who were considering the purchase of their first motorcycle, all of the Japanese and European manufacturers seized the opportunity to design and bring to market really cool, fun looking sports and adventure bikes that met those new restrictions, capturing those entry level riders and giving them a path of easy progression through their entire range of motorcycles. Riders for life.

Harley does none of these things.

Product development has stalled. And here is the paradox. It isn't that Harley Davidson doesn't want to innovate or improve. It is because when it tries, it is the very customer base that refuses to buy the new product. Even if that new Harley is lighter, faster, better in every way, and less likely to initiate the infamous Dyna death wobble and throw its rider into the path of oncoming traffic. Harley riders just want to buy Harleys. Big, fat, heavy, old-fashioned Harleys.

And new international markets? No sirree. Reagan killed that when he decided to give Harley Davidson an unfair advantage in trade tariffs to ensure that Harleys would always be built in the good old US of A. In response for manipulating the markets, Europe imposed strict and punitive import trade tariffs that means Harley can no longer compete anywhere outside the United States of America. Even Donald Trump, when president, called Harley out for that one.

The Harley Davidson that we see today is essentially the same Harley Davidson of five decades ago. A 1970s dinosaur. An unwieldy metaphor of styling, sound, and a desperate, *desperate,* longing for a time, a youthfulness, and a belief in a culture that really only ever was a knee-jerk reaction to rebelling against the other 99%.

And that is the biggest problem facing Harley Davidson. Its riders bought into the philosophy it sold over fifty years ago. It has failed to engage, or even attempt to recruit a new generation. Its riders are ageing out of the need to ever ride a motorcycle again. In truth, their next motorized purchase is more likely to be a mobility scooter.

Having been desperate enough to have climbed through a toilet window, I found myself back on the packed and constantly jostling street. I sighed and looked about me. This just wasn't my scene.

There were a few tough looking guys who wore the colours, but by a very long margin, most of these guys were dentists, family lawyers, accountants, milkmen, and like Mike, Mike and Donald back there, software salesmen.

In a rally that was supposed to represent the 1% I was surrounded by the 99.

Most folks here just enjoyed the look. The mystique. The culture. The music. The companionship.

And hey! Don't get me wrong. That is perfectly fine. I understand it. I actually fucking dig it. It's a cool thing to do. To be part of something so iconic and to do it all clad in assless chaps and shiny chains. Part of me genuinely craved to be part of it. A much, much taller and hirsute version of myself. One who would not look such an utter wanker in a bandana.

But to be honest, motorcycle choice aside there were just too many people at Sturgis. And not one of them my people. I had never felt so British and so alone in such a vast noisy sea of hairy heads, the top of my shiny dome barely level with the plethora of pale slabs of sweaty, meaty, tattooed arms.

The town was just too manic. I also didn't have any camping equipment with me and the chances of finding a bed for the night were zero to none. I had been enjoying my own company for far too long, and just didn't want to sacrifice the freedom that had bestowed.

I walked down the crowded street to stretch my map across the tank of the dusty bike. There was a small town only thirty miles north called Newell. It was far enough from Sturgis to be empty, and it looked large enough to have at least one Motel cheap and nasty enough to meet my needs.

I took one last circuit of the madly partying town and then headed first east and then north on State Road 79, turning my back on Sturgis and its mania with all things Harley and freedom.

Fargo

The sun was just beginning to slip from the sky when I pulled into the Conoco gas station on the southern outskirts of Newell. Next door to the gas station was a small restaurant, the Blue Line Diner. It looked more like a storage facility than an eatery from the outside, but I nonetheless marked it as a potential for dinner if I could find nothing else in the town.

There wasn't much to Newell. A few clapboard houses, the obligatory white pillared Baptist church and a low-lying high school that had an oversize billboard outside that proudly proclaimed the football team to be, '*Home of the Irrigators,*' which was puzzling to me. The United States of America is a nation obsessed with its sports teams being named after apex predators like The Panthers, The Wildcats and The Eagles.

You very rarely saw one named after an actual sedentary or prey animal such as The Lemmings, or The Sloths, or even less likely something janitorial like The Blackboard Wipers or The Pencil Sharpeners.

It turns out that the entire town of Newell was created and named after one Frederick Newell who, in 1902 was tasked by President Roosevelt with reclaiming vast swathes of arid dusty land through the creation of dams and irrigation channels, to transform the existing barren desert they found themselves in, into a bounteous garden of Eden.

When football teams come to play 'The Gators' in Newell, they know it isn't a team named after a big green snappy reptile, but rather a particularly singular man who directed the digging of over five-hundred miles of irrigation ditch. GO IRRIGATORS!

At the top end of the main street, I came to a stop sign and duly did. My map told me I needed to make a right turn, but that would take me towards the outskirts of the town and not having seen any sign of accommodation I was loathe to keep riding any further.

The alternative route was the road in front of me. It was dusty and abandoned. It ran in one straight line until it disappeared over the horizon surrounded on each side by rolling fields of corn and alfalfa.

With a sigh of resignation, I surrendered to the fact that I might have quite a few more miles to ride. I turned right onto the High Plains Main Street and there it was. The High Plains Inn. And right next to it the High Plain Restaurant. Folks are mighty proud of the High Plains in those thar parts.

The High Plains Inn looked like the Sunset Motel prior to it being renovated, so I didn't hold out much hope, but the lady on reception was Midwest friendliness personified. She gave me my key, told me where I could safely leave the bike, and pointed me to my room.

The room was spotless and comfortable, and I threw my bags onto the comfy bed with glee and ten minutes later I was clothed in cleanish jeans and my least grubby t-shirt, showered, and smiling.

The diner next door was simple, good home cooked food. Just what I wanted. I ordered the ribeye and when it came it was perfectly medium rare, served with some collard greens and the ubiquitous and irrefusable corn on the cob. As usual I ordered more beer than my dehydrated body was capable of processing.

I stepped back outside into the warm night air. I startled some bats that were gorging on the insects drawn to the sodium streetlights, by nearly toppling over into a really badly placed irrigation ditch some stupid bastard from the very early years of the twentieth century had carelessly left lying around.

I emitted a little scream and barely recovered by windmilling my arms and venting a hearty belch that luckily propelled me back, safely in the direction of my motel room.

I awoke early. I had another long ride ahead of me and had no expectations that I would stumble upon another hidden Badlands. Today would be a trial of tedium across the Great Plains, north to my final state on this soon to be finally-ending trip to Fargo in North Dakota.

There was no breakfast to steal, so in the half-light of a new morning I packed the bike. My boss had texted me during the night asking when I could be back in the office. Luckily my flight home was that evening so I texted him back to say I would meet him for lunch the following day.

I texted Paula to let her know I was on schedule to be back at the Atlanta Hartsfield-Jackson airport around nine-thirty that night and hit the road.

The road took me northeast along a road framed by gently waving corn for the first fifty or sixty miles and then dwindled to leave behind a dusty landscape more featureless than the moon. No more crops here, I figured I had finally slipped beyond the reach of '*The Irrigators.*'

Brown tussocky grasslands that once would have been home to a million, roaming bison stretched out on all sides away from me to touch each distant horizon.

There weren't even any habitations here. The first town I encountered was more than seventy-five miles from Newell. It was a town called Faith. I could only assume it had been named such by the pilgrims, whose stagecoach broke down there, because they still had sufficient faith that someone would come and rescue them from this tumbleweed strewn hellhole.

At Dupree I turned north and entered the Standing Rock Indian Reservation. The reservation covers over 3,500 square miles but has only 8,000 residents, mainly of the Hunkpapa and Sihasapa tribes.

The land remained flat and almost without feature. The road lay like an unfurled and perfectly straight ribbon of black velvet in front of me. I hunkered down and with only my own few thoughts to keep me company I fought to remain focussed on the ride and to eat up the fast miles and the slow passage of time.

Close to the town of McIntosh I almost suffered a bout of sensory overload as I had to negotiate first a left turn onto state road 12, and then only a few hundred yards later a right turn back on state road 65. My heart fairly palpitated with the thrill. It was all just too much excitement for me and suddenly I needed to pee quite badly.

I thought that I would take the opportunity to find a coffee shop in the small nearby town and stretch my legs. I rode all the way through town and then back again, but apart from the bank I saw nothing that looked like it might have both a coffee machine and a toilet so headed back to the main road to fill up with gas and empty my bladder at the Marathon gas station.

Back on State Road 65, and only a few miles later I crossed out of South Dakota and into North Dakota. I was nearly done with this endless ride.

It was there that I caught my first sight of the storm. It was a distant but threatening smudge on the very edge of the horizon west of me, but as I rode north it slowly grew until the sky split like ruined mayonnaise. To the east, sunshine, and clear blue. To the west — darkest midnight.

The area I was riding through was the northern part of Tornado Alley. Only the year before there had been three hundred and ninety-two tornados in this area over a very turbulent fourteen-day period.

The total number of tornados that occur in this region are somewhat predictable by skilled meteorologists. But the elemental nature of a tornado is predictably unpredictable.

The supercell thunderstorm was on an intersection with me, that much was clear. I could see lightning forking through the lighter upper clouds, and from beneath, gigantic thunderheads issued a heavy, grey curtain of rain. The storm could be seen walking its slow but deliberate way across the plains in my direction. It wasn't a twister yet but there were the first clear signs of rotation at the storms base where it scoured the plains into a plume of billowing dust across the barren grasslands.

There was nowhere to shelter. From curving horizon to curving horizon in every direction, nothing in sight stood more than three feet from the ground. Mounted as I was on the Ducati I might have been the tallest thing ever witnessed in South Dakota.

The road ran straight on. There seemed to be no alternative path to take that might lead me away from a drenching, and potentially being sucked up into the air like a cow from a barn and deposited in Oz like Dorothy and Toto.

It looked like our paths were destined to cross just to the north of the town of Raleigh. The atmosphere was charged, and all other sounds seemed supressed by the weight of the air around me. My ears popped against the pressure of the storm and the first spots of rain could be seen on the steaming tarmac and against the visor of my helmet. I rolled the throttle back just as a crack of lightning struck the ground off to my left. The darkness was lifted for a millisecond, and my retina was imprinted by the brilliant arc of electric blue light. I blinked several times, but the persistent bright spots would not yield from my vision.

The first gusts of the preceding storm front began to rock the bike. Clouds of disturbed dust flew past me, creating a thick paste where it merged with the increasing rain drops on my visor. Another lightning strike turned my world electric blue, matched in intensity half a second later by the loudest KERRRACKK of thunder I had ever heard.

I saw a dirt track on the map. It was labelled 84 and because it led east, directly away from the stormfront, I braked hard. I hadn't realised that I had ABS on the Ducati, such wonderful technology certainly didn't exist on the last bike I had owned, but the unfamiliar judder from the rear brake assured me that it was so, and I swung the Scrambler down what was really nothing more than a farm track.

The road led me past a long bank of grain silos. It was dusty and very bumpy, but the little Ducati handled the tractor ruts and patches with ease. I stood up on the foot pegs and managed to keep up a decent pace, at least as fast as the swift swirling front of the storm. Slowly the patter of rain from the leading edge of the storm began to slow and then abated. I was riding into clear weather, and I could see now, in the madly vibrating handlebar mounted mirrors, the bulk of the weather continuing to slip away to the north, the plume of dust behind me now replaced by the one kicked up only by my own steady progress.

I took a left turn, still on the dirt track and thirty-five minutes later, with a little whoop of delight at my cleverness I entered the small, but perfectly manicured town of Flasher. I passed a neatly maintained cemetery and then got back onto paved roads by the small post office. At the stop sign I saw a large banner for the Flasher public high school. I wasn't sure if the sign was a warning or an invitation, but the police cruiser parked in the parking lot made up my mind for me, and I made a quick right turn onto Highway 21.

Around eleven, after almost five hours of riding I crossed the Missouri River again, this time on the Grant March Bridge, the town of Mandan on the west side of the river and the town of Bismark on the east. The Missouri river was still surprisingly wide here. A flat dark green smudge sandwiched between the lush hills.

At precisely three in the afternoon, after an almost seven hours ride, I found myself on the outskirts of the city of Fargo. I gave out a little with a whoop of relief and delight, and almost immediately parked the popping and pinging Ducati outside the Fargo visitor's centre. I was almost done with my ride. I just had one remaining tick to put in my box of the things I wanted to see and do in the 'roads less travelled and things most people don't bother travelling to see' category of US Midwest states.

Fargo North Dakota isn't famous for many things. The only thing I knew about the town, which had drawn me nonetheless to attempt the ride, was its star billing in the 1996 film Fargo. In that film there is a famous scene where a body gets fed into a woodchipper.

And guess what's stood outside the visitor's centre? The actual woodchipper from the film itself! You can even pop inside and grab an artificial leg and a trapper's hat and have your picture taken feeding the leg into the mouth of the chipper. Which is exactly what I did next.

After getting the iconic photo taken, I returned both the artificial, fake blood covered stump and the trapper's hat to the visitors' centre. As I handed back the hat I began to wonder, perhaps too late, how many visitor's heads the hat had been pulled onto and how many generations of lice it had long been home to.

I ran both hands across my bald scalp with sudden revulsion and then pulled on my helmet and rode off towards town.

Fargo is a strange little place. Like much of the Midwest, it is an oasis of a town stranded and surrounded by the flattest, most featureless farmland in the world. Fargo could be twinned with the Russian Steppes, except the Steppes possess more hills, charm, and entertaining distractions.

Fargo was named after William Fargo, the founder of Wells Fargo and was once the divorce capital of the USA due to its lenient laws regarding such things. Other than the woodchipper, the town seemed to be doing well. The downtown was busy, and students walked the streets, drinking coffee and shopping which is always a good sign.

On the way into town, I pulled into a nearby garage and slowly but carefully hosed the nine states of mud and dust off the Ducati Scrambler. I polished her until she shone. I filled her up with gas, checked the tire pressures and adjusted the chain. I then used the filthy single bathroom to change out of my tatty riding gear and rode her up to the north of that city in the middle of absolutely bum-fuck nowhere.

I found the house I was looking for in the suburb of Horace Mann, not too many blocks from the university. I rode the bike up the neat concrete drive. The owner heard my arrival and rushed out, ridiculously pleased to see me.

He invited me inside and we had a cup of coffee together while I handed over the keys and the paperwork. He shared that he had been absolutely certain he would never see his purchase in one piece, and was genuinely thrilled to find this tired looking, grey bearded old English chap seated on his sofa with his new Ducati parked safely on his drive.

I summoned an Uber while I finished my coffee and then, thirty minutes later, back at the airport, I sat in the tiny departure lounge sipping a beer, with all of my gear around me waiting for my connecting flight to Minneapolis and then onwards back to Atlanta.

I took a long draught and wondered, as I often did at the end of a long bike ride, what on earth had possessed me to do what I had just done.

What Bike!

I drove into the office the next day to meet with my boss. He showed some concern as to why I was looking so thin and exhausted, with wild eyes staring out of pale, hollowed cheekbones. I explained that I had just ridden a motorcycle across nine states in eight days and he nodded in mute understanding. He was aware, at this point of our relationship, of my inability to control my more dangerous impulses.

We discussed work and a date for my retirement. I was only in my mid-fifties but had had enough of corporate work. I told my boss that there was no longer sufficient work to keep me employed, my colleagues had picked up close to all of my responsibilities at that point, so I was genuinely being paid to click my heels and stare out of the window. Apart from this meeting, I wasn't even really going into the office anymore.

My boss told me not to worry. Told me to take the money and keep my head down for a few months. Enjoy the free time. I was extremely fortunate I realise that, but just sitting around and doing nothing while being paid didn't sit quite right with me either.

A thought had occurred to me, the beginnings of a cunning plan.

"How about I offer some free consultancy to some of our biggest west coast customers?"

"Go on."

"I do a road trip. One last time. Start in Los Angeles and then work my way back towards Atlanta. Do a health check of the software our customers have already bought and see if I can spot some opportunities to sell them any more of our crap. It will keep me busy. You and I can justify the company paying me for a few more months, and we might even make a few more bucks out of the base."

My boss sat looking at me for a good minute and a half, his head cocked and a semi-amused expression on his face.

"OK. Draw up a plan for me. Let me know who, where, and when and I will approve it."

Back at home I discussed my idea with Paula.

"OK. But that's a lot of flights. I thought that's what you wanted to get away from."

"Yeah…but what if I didn't fly? What if…bear with me here." I cleared my throat and gave a little cough. I involuntarily touched the end of my nose which was a sure and certain 'tell' that I was uncertain as to the outcome of this conversation. I never could play poker and Paula's green eyes narrowed dangerously. But I was now committed to my path.

"What if…instead. I flew once. Out to the west coast, picked up a bike and then rode it home?"

"But that's…*miles*. Thousands probably…"

I could actually see the copper penny flipping end over end in the air in front of her. I saw the penny slowly drop to the ground to make a metallic rattling, settling sound as it came to rest tails up.

Her brow furrowed in the worrying manner that warned me after over thirty years of marriage that I had entered into uncertain and potentially perilous territory.

"Wait. Bike! Exactly *what* bloody bike are you talking about?"

"Well, now then my sweet. Absolute love of my life. My darling and most delightful English rose bud. Now that you come to ask. I thought that if I did some research,

I might find a little bike that I thought I might...you know..." I felt the need to clear my throat again. "Buy..."

"Buy!"

"Yeah. I won't spend much. Honest. I'll get a little belter. A bargain."

"But what about visiting Ben in A school? And then there's the day he sets sail from Jacksonville. We told him we would both be there."

"And we will. I can be in both places. I promise. You can even join me for as much of the ride as you want."

"Well, it seems you have it all planned already," and with that she turned her back and walked away.

I didn't actually have it all planned. But with permission granted, albeit somewhat tacitly, it was time to get started.

I had already begun to list out some of the places I had still not had the chance to visit, and now I began in earnest to make a mental map of my route. With a guilty glance over my shoulder, I also opened a Google browser window on my Mac and began the search for a suitable motorcycle.

The first bike I discounted was the Ducati Scrambler. I had enjoyed it greatly and it had instilled in me, once more, my nearly life-long love of motorcycling. I owed it so much for taking good care of me on my first hesitant miles and the subsequent charge north across the United States.

But it was a thug. Too much power for its weight. It destroyed back tires and wasn't comfortable enough or capable of carrying sufficient luggage for the journey that was forming in my mind's eye.

I began to research adventure bikes. Adventure bikes have existed for a long time, but back when I was doing some of my bigger trips in the 1980s and 1990s, they had been the exclusive domain of serious rallies and riders like Hubert Auriol and Edi Orioli at the Dakar. Enormously tall and heavy bikes, with gigantic fuel tanks, long travel suspension and knobbly tires, capable of crossing deserts and fording rivers with equal ease.

I was surprised to see that the industry had been incredibly successful in taming and modifying bikes like the KTM 450 Rally and the iconic XT600 Ténéré and morphing them into an all-purpose motorcycle that could be ridden by almost anybody on a mix of terrains.

I did some more research on YouTube and was genuinely astonished to find that, if you believe the hype, pretty much everybody was now riding a BMW R1250GS or a KTM 1290 Super Adventure around the world and vlogging every moment of their journey to thousands of interested followers.

I think in all of my more modest trips combined I only took a total of thirty grainy photos and had to wait a fortnight for Pronto Print to have them ready for pick up. Of all of the miles I rode from Southport to Istanbul I have a total of three surviving photographs.

Time had certainly moved on, and not at all in a bad way. A trip the magnitude of world circumnavigation was once the domain of the privileged or the demented, or in Ted Simon's case, perhaps both.

I went around some of the local dealers and took the time to inspect some of the options. Many of the most popular adventure bikes were all much too big and tall for me. I took a trial sit on the BMW R1200GS. It took me three, huffing and puffing heaves to rock it upright from the side stand, only to have it almost topple over the other way and crush me like a grape.

It took me several days and the reading of reviews on that interweb thing and hours of watching 'influencers' on YouTube to decide on the right and proper choice of bike.

The research all finally came out in favour of a Suzuki 650 V-Strom. I thought it an odd name but then found out that the V obviously denotes the V-twin nature of the bike and Strom is German for stream.

The bike looked to be about the right size. It would pull well enough one up, and even do some limited two up touring if my darling wife would ever speak to me again and join me on the journey. The V-Strom didn't seem to be the most capable adventurer off road, but the only time you would find me riding off road would be if I had already crashed, so I didn't consider that to be an insurmountable problem.

I did some further research and found a good, higher mileage example for sale at a verry good price, located at a Suzuki dealership in Los Angeles.

San Diego

The Delta Boeing 737 landed in LAX with a loud screech of tires. I awoke with the strange combination of a wide yawn and the flutter of butterflies in my stomach. The plans had been drawn up. I had called the dealership and they had serviced, cleaned and prepared the bike for me.

I got an Uber for the short drive out to Hawthorne where the dealer was located, all of my gear stashed in an overstuffed rucksack, that once emptied would pack flat.

The 2016 Suzuki V-Strom 650 positively gleamed, bright red and polished aluminium, reflecting back at me that uniquely bright and smog filtered quality, of yet another sunny day in Los Angeles.

The bike had travelled a decent 34,000 miles but it had a full-service history and the dealer promised me it had just been fully serviced once more. As I approached the bike, I took a quick glance at the seat height. The V-Strom was only a 650 but it was still so intimidatingly tall. I wasn't one-hundred-percent certain I could get my creaking hips to flex high enough to throw a leg over the seat successfully.

The bike had Suzuki panniers and top box already fitted so, while the dealer fannied about in the office with the bounteous amount of paperwork that is required to buy anything with an engine in America, I distributed my few belongings between the available spaces.

With all of the paperwork completed and my payment made, I stashed the spare set of keys into the top box and swallowed hard as the salesman patted me on the back and then stood back to watch me leave.

I wished with all of my heart that he would just fuck off back inside and leave me alone to either ride off, easy rider like into the sunset, or to fail to clear the seat height with a stiff leg and end up, flat on my back in the dust of the car park.

With no other choice, I cinched up the helmet strap and keeping the bike resting on the side stand I managed, with a worryingly loud click of a hip, to get my right leg across the seat. I swung up the side stand, the bike easily levered upright to be balanced on the tippiest of toes.

I pulled in the clutch, checked the unfamiliar display to make sure I was in neutral and fired up the bike. I blipped the throttle and watched with joy as the analogue needle swept across the tacho. The gearbox gave a familiar and satisfying Suzuki clunk as I toed the bike into first gear, and I carefully slipped the clutch to turn out of the dealership's car park. The bike was as torquey as I had hoped, it felt like there was a big barrel of low-end grunt just waiting to be unleashed.

The riding position was comfortably upright, and the tall screen threw the warm afternoon wind over the top of my helmet. On the move the bike lost its initially intimidating height, in fact at speed the visibility gained was a godsend. I could see easily over other cars and scan the road beyond for hazards and overtaking opportunities. It was easy to flick left and right, an absolute joy to ride. The gearbox was slicker than a second-hand car salesman's patter and the throttle response smooth and predictable.

I made a right at the end of West Olive Street and merged a little tentatively onto the perennially busy La Cienega Boulevard. I immediately headed south to get as far away from the city as quickly as I was able.

I had my first customer meeting in Irvine just south of the city and then I planned to ride back west to meet up with Paula and some old friends in Laguna Beach. Paula was already there, waiting for me. After I had shown her the route I planned to ride, and some of the cool places I wanted to visit, her demeanour had changed a little, and she had decided to accompany me for a few days here and there along the route, picking out the best of the best sightseeing stops, and then jetting back to Atlanta to avoid the long and arduous riding bits that she was well aware were sure to somehow creep into all of my motorcycle based travel itineraries.

I parked the bike in the shade of a towering palm in the car park of my intended customer and stowed and locked my helmet and riding jacket in the top box. I turned on my phone and saw that I had a voicemail from my boss. I called him up.

"Hey. Thanks for calling me back, Andy. I hate to tell you this, but the company just let me go."

"What! What the hell."

"It's fine. I'll find something else. I was already looking anyway."

"But what about..."

"You? Don't worry about you. The senior management team will continue to shake things up some, but they are a shambles. I will make sure that they will honour your retirement date. Cancel any of those customer meeting we talked about and just keep your head down like I told you to. Keep taking the salary for the next few months. Enjoy yourself."

And with that the line went dead.

I stood in the delicate light of the Californian afternoon. It was breezy and a chill blew in from the coast. I called my contact at the company in whose car park I was already parked and told him that something unforeseen had just come up, and that I could no longer make the meeting. It was no big deal. We were friends and we were probably just going to catch up and drink a coffee together anyway. He told me to take care and hoped that whatever the issue had been would soon be resolved and we hung up.

I was a free man. No. Much better than that. I was free man with the gift of both time on his hands and a salary still being paid into his bank account. At least for a while anyway.

With a broad and goofy grin on my face, I took CA-133 back towards the coast. The V-Strom ran smooth and fast, away from the smog and clutter of LA.

California was a series of soft rolling hills, a pleasant and cool country filled with grass covered bluffs amid a pastel sky. For some reason this part of the world always evoked scenes of those early pioneers of the old west for me. Scenes of covered wagons filled with families and every manner of household items, rattling, and creaking the last few miles to reach the coast.

For those first settlers, testy and single-minded enough, to ride a wagon and horses across the formidably lofty and craggy peaks of the Rockies, the first virginal touch of those hills and that first tangy salt-scented snifter of the ocean must have seemed like paradise attained.

Most pioneers in the middle years of the nineteenth century took the famed Oregon Trail to reach California. The route was entirely logical. It mostly followed rivers and the valleys they had carved to finally cross the Rocky Mountains at a location known as South Pass in Wyoming. South Pass is at a lofty elevation of almost a mile and a half, but it is still the lowest part of the continental divide and the easiest route for any wagon and horses.

A good team of horses could make, on average, fifteen miles a day. The entire journey, from east to west took between four and six months. The draw of the west, for most colonists, before news was made of the Gold that would soon be found in them thar hills, was the fervent and almost romantically hysterical concept of a '*manifest destiny*' a belief that their infallible Christian God had issued a mandate that the west belonged to them, and them alone, and that it must be settled to allow Christianity and the good word to be spread across its bounteous and munificent lands.

Filled by religious fervour to do their God's bidding, and following on from the success of previous pioneers, a group of eighty-seven men, women and children, that would soon become known as the Donner Party, set out from Springfield Illinois in the spring of 1846 with the same goal in mind – to continue the settlement of the promised land and to convert the heathen natives. There were souls to save! Can I hear a Halleluyah?

Unfortunately for them, things did not go so well. They were recommended a different route by their guide. It was called the Hastings Route, and it crossed the lofty and jagged Wasatch Range of the Rocky Mountains, before then crossing the Great Salt Lake Desert and then the Sierra Nevada's.

Even contemplating that route today, with the aid of satellite navigation, up to date maps, Google and a powerful four-wheel drive car, and perhaps a small helicopter, at my disposal, it didn't look or sound like the most auspicious route. And so, it proved to be for the Donner Party.

Things went badly almost from the get-go. Heavy rains and rising rivers slowed their initial progress. This in an era, where the crossing could take up to six months, any delay could mean hitting parts of the route in winter rather than summer or fall.

Divisions immediately broke out in their ranks. The Wasatch range proved to be much more difficult to cross than they had been led to believe. Unlike the Oregon Trail that, lofty though it might be, at least carried a fair amount of traffic and was well navigated and marked, the path over the Wastach was little travelled by anybody other than the Native American populations. It meant that every day, mile after mile, trees had to be felled, boulders had to be broken and then manually levered into valleys far below in order to allow the teams to pass. Wagon drivers had to continuously take care to lock wheels at each pause in the journey, to stop the wagons from rolling back down the precipitously steep paths, to be instantly turned into huge piles of kindling and canvas on the rocks far below, taking the horses to their doom with them.

By the time they came down from the mountains, most of their water had gone, their horses were fatigued and lame, and food was already running short.

This did not bode well, because in front of them lay the seemingly endless desert of the salt flats. It took the party six days and six nights to cross the desert. At night, the temperature dropped precipitously and froze the sands.

In the blistering heat of the day, as the sun rose high into the sky, the moisture underneath the salt crust rose to the quickly thawing surface and turned it into a soft and claggy mud that clogged the hooves of the horses and pulled the wagons down and into its oozing embrace.

The wagon wheels sank, in some cases up to the hubs. Horses and cattle became stranded, some so weakened and dehydrated they had to be abandoned, still yoked to their wagons, and simply left to die.

With the hellscape of the flats behind them, the remainder of the party still faced one last push, to cross the Sierra Nevada's. This crossing proved even more challenging than the Wasatch range. The mountains were just too steep for the wagons. To curse them further, a full month before winter was due, a snowstorm lasting eight days stopped them dead in their tracks.

The survivors made a desperate emergency camp at a desolate place called Trucklee Lake. Short of both food and water they had no choice but to wait out the storm. With barely sufficient food for the settlers, the horses and oxen soon began to die. Their corpses were initially piled up and frozen. But as the storm continued, they were all slowly eaten by the now starving group.

The food situation became so dire that families began to eat the ox hide rugs that kept them warm, and even the ox hide that lined the roofs of the wagons that kept them dry were stripped and used as a thoroughly gnawable but non-nutritious food source.

It wasn't long before the pioneers were forced to resort to cannibalism to survive. Initially they ate the bodies of those who had succumbed to starvation, sickness or extreme cold, but it is documented that at least two Native American guides were deliberately murdered so that the Europeans could survive.

In the end, only forty-eight of the eighty-seven pioneers, along with three very ornery mules made it all the way to California.

The thought of those exhausted and starving pioneers made me feel a touch peckish myself, so I pulled into the next roadside Del Taco and sat in the car park, enjoying the sunshine, while hot sauce dripped down the front of my riding jacket from the overstuffed bean and beef burrito I had ordered.

I rode down the Laguna Canyon Road in the late afternoon sunshine. As I got closer and closer to the coast, the low hills morphed into craggy cliffs. Insanely expensive white stucco houses clung to the hills supported by rickety looking stilts. Avant Garde restaurants and bohemian art galleries lined both sides of the busy street that cut its way through the canyon.

The amount of traffic slowly increased around me, and my speed slowed until I hit a red light at a large and busy T-junction. In front of me was suddenly unveiled the wide blue spread of the Pacific Ocean, framed by a pretty crescent of cool golden sand that curved around the bay. I made a left, rode down the busy street a few hundred yards, and pulled into the car park of the historic Hotel Laguna.

The hotel is billed as a *'Grand Old Lady'* that has graced the scene for over one hundred and twenty-five years. And judging by the shocking state of the plumbing in the rooms this is almost true. But the building that I was drinking a cold Stella in that day with my wife and two of our best friends is about as original as *'Trigger's broom.'*

The original hotel burnt to the ground only sixty days after opening. The hotel was rebuilt but then moved to its current location in the early 1900s. It was again demolished and completely rebuilt in 1928. It was this version of the hotel that we spent the night in.

In our large but somewhat, shall we say originally featured room, I opened a window to get some air and then immediately regretted it because I found that now opened, it refused to close. In the bathroom the tap squirted water out of the faucets at an angle so jaunty that it drenched my crotch making me appear, not for the first time, that I had pissed myself. In the bedroom the floorboards creaked alarmingly. If you happened, during the course of the night, to lose your marbles, not to worry, you would find them all rolled together, in a tight little group, in the very south-eastern corner of the room.

But. Walk out the back of the hotel and you can still see why Humphrey Bogart and Errol Flynn used to frequent the hotel, and why patrons still flock to its white painted Spanish arched architecture and lofty, and bell less, bell tower. The hotel sits directly on the sands of the beach on some of the most expensive real estate in the world. At night the lights of 'The Laguna' twinkle, and the moonlit white flecked breakers can be seen and heard to crash relentlessly onto the cool sands of the shore.

In the morning Paula and our friends jumped into their car and headed out to Palm Springs. I would join them later in the day, but first I had a diversion. I wanted to ride part of the Pacific Coast Highway down towards San Diego to the border with Mexico.

I had mentioned the possibility of a quick run down the coast to San Diego while having a drink or two with a few Californian friends. Upon hearing the news, their cool and laid-back bohemian chic had immediately been displaced by the doom and gloom typical of a group of late middle aged British dads discussing the possibility of a rainy trip to the Birmingham NEC on a bank holiday Monday.

San Diego was only seventy-two miles away, but the comments all went along the lines of:

"You should have set off before we had this conversation if you wanted to avoid the traffic."

"You're not using I-5, are you? You are? Well then, you deserve everything you get."

"It will take you *days* to get there."

"Don't go!"

Perhaps I was lucky, but apart from having to slow down once or twice for the inevitable roadworks, the ride south was easy and relaxing, the gleaming Pacific Ocean was an almost constant companion to my right. The V-Strom pulled from low range like an express train and sat at seventy miles an hour easily, the big V-twin engine thumping away easily beneath me, sun flashing from my visor, as I passed palm tree after palm tree.

Juniper trees, violet Jacarandas, and sand bluffs whizzed by as the sun rose in the sky. The land that that would soon become named California was originally owned by the Spanish of course, and most of the names of the towns in the state still reflect that early history.

In 1821, after the Mexican War of Independence, Spain reluctantly handed the state of California to Mexico. At that time, the residents of California felt that Spain's trade monopoly had been largely to the detriment of the community and were actually very keen to join with its southern neighbour.

In 1846 the United States decided that it would also quite like the territory for itself and invaded as part of the Bear Flag Revolt which gave the state the emblem that still graces its state flag today. War between the United States and Mexico broke out and was fought across several skirmishes for the next year or so before Mexico finally ceded the new state of California to the USA.

It is easy to make the mistake, from a modern perspective, to wonder why California changed hands so much and so easily. Why didn't countries fight harder to retain ownership of such a valuable jewel of real estate? But in the mid-nineteenth century, California was just a mix of arid, barren desert and wild trails. Despite the proximity to the Pacific Ocean, it was sparsely populated and produced almost no usable crops, had no natural resources, or other useful industry. Both Spain, and then Mexico were actually quite eager to let it go.

The Treaty of Guadalupe Hidalgo was signed on February 2, 1848. What is rather uncanny, is that a mere seven days later, gold was discovered in the newest state in the union in the burgeoning United States of America

Mexico would surely have put up more of a fight had it known that the Great Californian Gold Rush was about to become part of history and the changing fortunes and finances of California.

It's almost as though one of those pesky Yankees knew something the Mexicans didn't.

One notable exception to all of the Spanish place names made me chuckle inside my helmet. Amongst all of the San Clementes, Del Rays, Solanas and Encinitas, I passed by a town called Cardiff-by-the-Sea. I found out later that it was named by a chap called Frank Cullen who, having bought a plot of land in 1875, that looked out over the sun-kissed, azure Pacific Ocean, for the princely sum of thirty-dollars, decided he still missed the leaden skies, horizontal freezing rains, and mud-filled estuary of his native Wales, and named his new town after his ancestral home.

I pulled into San Diego just in time for lunch. I rode slowly through the Gaslamp district, full of high-end bars, clubs, and cocktail lounges, and then out across the insanely pretty Coronado Bridge, the city skyline behind me and the large Naval Station to my left, the bay a cluster of madly glittering diamond shards under the bright glare of the midday sun.

I parked the bike beneath the shade of a fan palm and shook off my sweaty riding gear to take a table outside on the patio of the spectacular Hotel Coronado. I ate a buffalo chicken sandwich with fries and drank a cold beer while I relaxed, for a few minutes, just people watching and enjoying the heat of the day and the touch of the cool Pacific breeze on my bare skin.

After I had decorated my riding jacket and jeans with sufficient buffalo and ranch sauce to feed the occupants of a small Mexican town, I rode south down Monument Road to park the bike close to the public bathrooms in International Park. I wanted to take a look, for the first time in my life, at the United States border with Mexico.

It was an eerie and unsettling experience to see such a thing. A steel barrier that ran along the road and even for a few tens of yards out into the Pacific Ocean. This artificial barrier in the middle of a nature reserve and public beach, that arbitrarily controlled and decided who was allowed to get a tan sitting in the warm sands of those particular dunes, or who could dip their toes in that particular bit of the ocean.

I peered through the fence hoping to see something of Mexico. I even stood on a rock and jumped up and down a bit. But on my side of the wall the government had adopted that American staple of military officiousness it does so well with agencies such as the TSA and the IRS. The number of signs telling me to just to politely fuck off were plentiful and there wasn't much that I could see through the barrier, anyway, just the very top of a pretty Mexican lighthouse.

I found out later that at the base of the lighthouse, that stands in the town of Tijuana, right beside the steel border built by the United States is a piece of the Berlin Wall gifted to Mexico by the German government. The plaque next to it bears the hopeful and inspiring, but still clearly flawed sentiment, "*A World Without Walls.*"

It is the same piece of the Berlin Wall that then President Trump refused to accept several years before.

Ten minutes later I was back on the bike, leaving the coast and her chilling zephyrs behind me. I was headed to the desert and Palm Springs.

I took the Expressway north initially, just to clear the clutter of the city sprawl, but left its dullness and busyness at Temecula to cut across country on State Road 79. Gentle curves set amid a rolling scrubland led me up and into the hills. A row of distant mountains shimmered in the distant heat haze in front of me. The land slowly drifted into scrub and a flat and arid sandscape.

The temperature soared as I rode northeast, but then in the foothills of the Santa Rosa and San Jacinto mountains the road began to climb to leave the dust and scorching temperatures of the valley behind.

The ribbon of highway swept me around bend after bend, the road mostly empty, the little Suzuki powering easily out of each hairpin. I spent the first thirty minutes shifting all the way from second gear, all the way up to fifth gear and then, all the way back again as I swept through the grin inducing twisty bits.

I then had a revelation when I entered a sharp hairpin a tad too fast. I didn't have time to cog safely into second, so I was forced to bumble around in third. I thought the Suzuki would bog down, and don't get me wrong, the bike didn't accelerate as swiftly as it could have done on the exit, but the torquey engine pulled just fine in third. For the rest of the day, I barely changed out of third and fourth gear.

When I had first picked up the bike, I thought the completely upright riding position was...well...a bit old manish to be honest. Then I rode it a few more miles and finally caught my reflection in a shop window and realized that it was only me that made the bike look a bit old manish. The V-Strom was super cool. Powerful, adaptable, comfortable. Super easy, easy, easy to ride. I was having so much fun!

As I rode through deep canyons, the tall walls obscured any view. But the lack of a distracting landscape didn't matter. All of my attention was snared by matching the correct gear to the next bend, scrubbing speed, counter steering through the bend and then rolling the throttle back. The road carried me higher and higher and the cool of the almost eight-thousand feet of elevation suddenly began to chill me. On the distant peak to my right, I was surprised to still see that snow lay thick and perennially frigid.

Distant views were refused me until I rounded one more bend and came out on the top of the world. Naturalist John Muir wrote of the views from the peak, *'The view from San Jacinto is the most sublime spectacle to be found anywhere on this earth!'*

What is unusual here is the height and steepness of the mountains that surround the narrow Coachella Valley that lay like a rich Turkish tapestry suddenly unrolled and revealed below me.

The San Jacinto Mountain range tops out at a literally breath-taking eleven-thousand feet and the valley below is actually sixty-eight feet below sea level.

The valley between its lofty and sheer walls is a dead flat. The valley floor is a constant blur, shimmered into submission by the furnace of the desert heat that threatens to incinerate the very air.

The desert communities of Palm Springs, Palm Desert and Indian Wells were scattered like artificial emeralds, man-made oases created by constant irrigation, an endless battle against the encroachment and withering drought of the natural terrain.

The road was so steep on the Coachella side that it resembled an Alpine descent, but the V-Strom was an easy ride, not too powerful to get me into trouble when I got it right, but smooth and with sufficient grunt in those reliable third and fourth gears to grant me leniency if I got into a bend in the wrong gear.

With the peak behind me and the desert in front, the air temperature once more began to soar. By the time I got close to the valley floor it was already well over one-hundred and ten Fahrenheit. The temperature in the valley is a breathless, "somebody left the damn Bessemer Convertor door open again", type of heat.

I cracked the visor to get a little air and the oven of the day immediately rolled my lips back over teeth instantly transformed into something resembling a burnt picket fence. And my eyebrows burst into flames. At least that's what it felt like.

In Palm Springs I rode along the deserted main street. Where there were folks, they were seated in the bars and restaurants taking refuge from the punishment. Every patio had an outdoor cooling mister, spraying ice cold water to create a curtain of cool against the barrage of the day. I did my best to ride through the over spray, but it was impossible to avoid the heat completely. I couldn't figure out how the tarmac just didn't melt, I guess it was made out of barbeque briquettes or Space Shuttle tiles or something.

Luckily, I didn't have much further to ride. I found the hotel where Paula and our friends had booked for the night. I parked the bike in the shade and ran, vampire like, my jacket above my head, across the steaming car park and into the thundering cool of the air conditioning and the welcome of the hotel bar.

Kingman

I awoke early with a banging head. Bloody Stella Artois. I had had a few the night before, purely to rehydrate you understand. We had a room right by the hotel pool and had sat out watching the bats come out to hunt as the evening temperature plummeted into the high nineties.

With full darkness enveloping the mountains behind us, the family in the room next to ours had emerged. Like nocturnal bushbabies they appeared, blinking, and rubbing eyes. They had come from Wisconsin with young children, they explained, and hadn't realised that Palm Springs was owned and operated by Lucifer himself and kept at the same operating temperature as the eternally tormenting fires of the underworld. They had taken to hiding their pale bodies inside their darkened hotel room during the day, and then crawling out to let the kids play in the pool at midnight for an hour.

I had an early breakfast with Paula. I took five of the plastic bottles of water that were lined up by the coffee machine, sneaking them into my helmet along with two bread rolls and some honey sliced ham. It was all probably free for the guests to take, but I always got a little frisson of excitement at the thought of doing something illicit. At my age you take what thrills you can.

Back in the rapidly warming car park, I packed the bike and said goodbye to Paula once more. I was going to ride across the south side of Joshua Tree National Park and then, taking a couple of days, I would find my way to the south side of the Grand Canyon where we had another nice hotel booked. Paula would meet me there, so I could spare her the probably needless several hundred-mile detour, the inevitable stay in a shitty motel, and the sweating of literal buckets.

The sun was just creeping over the line of hills to the east. The soft light of the desert was spectacular in the truest sense of the word. Fan palms and cactus reached into the pastel toned sky while I enjoyed the briefest moments of the chill that remained from the relative cool of the desert night.

The Coachella was one of the most breath-taking places I have ever seen. The valley is entirely encircled by that formidable line of the distant, dusky, tall, snow-capped mountains. In the morning stillness they are painted lilac and ochre and blurred into the background by both distance and the slowly rising heat of the day. The valley captures the attention but also the spirit. It is one of the few places I have found on earth that insists that you stop. That you take the time to just stand still for a moment and truly look. If you get the opportunity, please go. The view are all spectacular, but the best view, in my humble opinion, is with a frosty glass of Stella Artois in hand looking out from the upstairs patio of the Tommy Bahamas Marlin Bar on North Palm Canyon Drive. It is perfect.

But, of course, in this mean old world, outside the wonder of nature there is usually a considerable price to be paid for such beauty.

The streets are broad and beautifully landscaped. Everything in the valley speaks of comfort and ease. But there is a good reason that the golf and country clubs in the valley don't post their joining fees. If you have to ask, you should already know that you are probably not welcome there. The restaurants are horrendously busy from six until seven in the evening and then empty quickly and completely.

The valley has become the dusty, creaky, geriatric home of the considerably elderly and the even more considerably wealthy. It is the *'Bide-a-While Rest Home'* of millionaires and would be billionaires. It is the retired playground of famous TV celebrities and ex-presidents. Everybody you meet will tell you that Bob Hope used to have a home here, and that Barack Obama still does.

I jumped onto I-10, not because I wanted to ride the interstate, but because there was no other road that would lead me east and out of the valley. The sky was the clearest of cornflower blues, criss-crossed only by the contrails of the jetliners heading towards Los Angeles to the west.

On either side of the highway was a wild country filled with tumbled rocks and tumble weeds. Low jagged hills clung to the horizon like sleeping, dust covered giants. They say that Montana is the big sky State, but I beg to differ.

I was riding, being drawn by the V-Twin, through a land of endless vistas that stretched the earth taut across a canvas painted with the delicate desert hues of bone white silica, the thousand shades of grinding sand, the crumbled stone, and the pale green and startling yellow buds of the occasional, scattered, Creosote Bush.

The vista was beautiful in its untamed and brutalist manner, but the little Suzuki seemed undaunted by neither the heat nor the distance.

Unlike myself. The temperature rose to wrap around me with all of the welcome of a heated blanket in a sauna. The sweat oozed from pores to drench me. My hands and feet, clothed in leather gloves and boots, were hotter than a rattlesnake's taint. Despite levering the visor open and making sure the vents were admitting as much speed cooled air as was possible, my head had already begun to pound.

At a bleak and desolate place called Desert Center, I turned off the interstate and took CA-177 north. The sun dazzled and rose like a furnace slowly into the sky. It dominated the sky, the glare blinding, and splintering into the multi-coloured shards of the prism as it touched each micro-scratch on my visor. The temperature soared and the sweat continued to trickle down every orifice I owned, and one or two that nature had just created. My mouth dried around a swollen tongue and even blinking became a gritty chore.

I turned east onto CA-62 and at yet another desolate place in the desert called Rice Desert Signpost, I stopped to take my helmet off and to drain a barely cold bottle of water in one very noisy, gurgling slurp.

Rice Desert Signpost is nothing more than a dusty pull off in the middle of absolutely nowhere. I saw a pole set in the broken earth. It looked all the world like a totem and my heart raced. I was intrigued, thinking that I might be the first to discover an actual Native American relic out here in the middle of nowhere.

On closer inspection I found that it was covered in colourful and home-made signs scribbled with the names of the towns, with mileages scrawled beneath, from which my fellow dusty travellers had begun their journeys.

I checked the map, and with the sun briskly turning my bald head the colour of a London bus, I screwed up my eyes to trace a finger across the ribbon of paper road, to see that I was finally getting close to the great Colorado River, the promise of a pleasant glimpse of something moist and blue before a turn to the north.

Forty-five minutes later I rode underneath the massive iron spans of the railway bridge and then across the cobalt blue serpent of the Colorado River. A few sparse trees lined the banks of the river on the Arizona side of the river, plunging desperate roots deep into the soil to reach its life-giving moisture.

The road followed the lazy meander of the river until I reached the southern tip of Lake Havasu. The lake is really a reservoir, formed when the Parker Dam was built across the Colorado River in 1938. Havasu is the Mojave word for blue. The Mojave tribes lived along the Colorado River until they were forced by the US Government to move to the Colorado River Reservation in 1865.

I took a quick look at the Dam itself. It is the deepest dam in the world apparently. But of course, by the very nature of dams, most of its depth, needed to reach the bedrock of the Colorado River, is under water. The bits of the dam that stood above the water were somewhat uninspiring. There was one cool thing about the dam. Standing dead centre of the dam, looking out, north, across the cobalt blue of the river, I stood with hands on hips, my left leg in California and my right leg in Arizona, which technically meant that I simultaneously had one testicle in both a different state and a different time zone from the other, the thought of which made me a little woozy with delight.

I glugged down two more of my bottles of water, hot enough now to make a nice cup of tea with, if I had thought to bring my Tetley's with me. I wiped the sweat from a sun puckered brow and clambered back on the bike to continue north, still sweating like an Arab at a Klan rally in the increasing heat of the day.

I was bound for Lake Havasu City for one reason only. Located in the middle of the desert is a little piece of

England. In 1968, Lake Havasu City's founder, Robert P. McCulloch saw an opportunity to bring a little tourism to the state of Arizona. He planned to build a new and unique town in the middle of the desert.

In my youth, I had been told an urban legend that an unscrupulous English conman had sold what some gullible America had believed to be London's iconic Tower Bridge, only for the said hapless American to find that what he had actually bought had been a fake.

The urban legend comes close, but the reality is that McCulloch knew exactly what he wanted and what he was buying. The London Bridge that he bought had been sinking slowly into the Thames for many years. The cost to repair was prohibitive, so, rather than demolish the bridge, the city sought to make some money out of the problem and sell the entire thing.

McCulloch was the man to buy it. He purchased the 18th century London Bridge and shipped it back, brick by numbered brick all the way back to Arizona. He even bought and shipped the ornate lamp posts, made from melted-down cannons, that lined and lit the bridge. Interestingly, the cannons were the same ones that had been captured by the British from Napoleon's army shortly after the battle of Waterloo in 1815.

The five arched spans of the bridge were painstakingly rebuilt and, because, back in Lake Havasu City there existed no natural span of water for the bridge to cross, McCulloch even went as far as to have a man-made river dredged so that water could flow beneath his creation.

Amazingly, because of his vision the city boomed, and 'London Bridge' became the second most popular tourism destination, bested only by the Grand Canyon, in the state of Arizona.

I parked the V-Strom by the English Village Fountain, a recreation of what somebody living in the middle of the desert, whose brain has been baked continuously by the maddening heat since birth, might imagine London to resemble. There was a little tea shop, a smattering of British flags and a bright red phone box. The fountain was surrounded by Trafalgar Monument type lions, squirting water from their raised throats into the fountain. It was all very sweet, if a little surreal.

In my head I adopted a cockney swagger, and with an accent as bad as Dick Van Dyke's, I had a quick French kiss in the bathrooms of the visitor's centre, and then took a ball and chalk across the field of wheat to have a butcher's hook at the bridge. Of course, it was a huge disappointment. It didn't look or feel like London at all.

It was just an old, but newly built bridge in the middle of Arizona. I could see what McCulloch was trying to achieve, and based on the success the city has enjoyed I guess I was content to be proven wrong. The American visitors certainly seemed to lap it all up. But the scene just didn't work for me, well...because the bridge is in the middle of a fucking *desert*, surrounded by sand, endless sunshine and palm trees.

If McCulloch had wanted his vision to be truly evocative of London and the era, he should have imported a ton of jellied-eels, a smattering of dog shit, some litter, and a flat-roofed pub where you could enjoy a pie and mash dinner, and then have a good-old fashioned punch up in the car park.

It was the middle of the day and standing on the bridge was like standing on a baking tray with the sun set to Gas Mark eight, so I bought a freshly chilled bottle of water, necked it in one long slug and walked back to the bike.

I followed the course of the Colorado River north and then took the slip road right to join I-40. The terrain remained rugged. Wild vegetation dotted the landscape, coarse and scrubby brush and thorny thicket, thick-skinned greenery immune to the arid conditions. Low hills loomed on the cloudy horizon, but the sun remained a constant dazzling siren high above me.

There was a railway line only a few hundred meters off to my right. It ran parallel to the highway for mile after mile. A huge diesel locomotive had been keeping pace with me since the town of Yucca. It must have been pulling thirty to forty huge, coloured wagons. It kept me company almost all the way to the town of Kingman, sometimes distant, sometimes within a few meters, until I finally turned off the interstate to look for a Motel that might meet my budget.

My choice seemed to be between two motels only separated by a short, scrubby stretch of desert on the historic Route 66 which runs directly through the town.

Choice one was the Ramblin Rose Motel, and choice two was the Rodeway Inn. Both had the classic single storey motel layouts, with the rooms accessed directly from the car park. I had learned my lesson by now, so I took a quick look at the reviews before I made my decision.

Rodeway Inn — "*Worst Hotel in the world - had a shower and then slept in my car.*"

Ramblin Rose — "*Primitive but clean.*"

I was still tempted by the Rodeway Inn despite the disparity in the reviews, partly due to the peculiarity of its name and because it had a pool. But I had no swimming trunks with me, so I opted for the safer option and spent forty-six bucks for a small, primitive but clean room at the Ramblin.

The room had the essentials and nothing more, although there was a large sign by reception that informed me that come the morning I would be enjoying a delicious free breakfast. Breakfast and helmet lunch I thought with a sly wink to myself, there being nobody else to wink to. I parked the bike as close to the bedroom door as I could and dragged my gear inside.

I haven't been to prison — yet — but the room provided a little insight into that particular life experience. The bed was small, but it still touched both the back wall and the front wall where the window was located. I had to clamber over it to reach the bathroom. If the night got hot, I could easily open the window and sleep with my feet dangling out into the parking lot.

The room had been recently cleaned but on the carpet by the side of the bed was what looked worryingly like the outline of a body drawn in chalk dust and hastily erased with the side of a shoe. The joys of staying in the independently owned and operated American Motel.

Kingman is a strange town. When travelling, especially solo, you can sometimes feel like you are travelling towards the end of world, and sometimes, as was now the case, you realise you may have arrived.

Kingman was named after Lewis Kingman, an engineer for the Atlantic and Pacific Railroad. The town began life as a primitive, backwater siding for the railroad and I think, it is fair to say, that it has retained this modest claim right up until the present day.

It wasn't without *some* small charms. I had a joyless and mostly inedible meal at a Chinese restaurant. I was the sole occupant. A rabid wolf pack would have struggled to gnaw the meat from the ribs and the Beef Mongolian looked like the chef had emptied a can of pedigree chum onto a plate of sperm. I ate it all anyway. I was really hungry.

With a rumbling stomach and a belch loud enough to set off a car alarm, I walked across the road to buy a pack of beers from a liquor store that was situated in the centre of a gigantic but mostly abandoned car park.

As I walked, alone and in the blackness of the night, I noticed a single car that was suspiciously parked thirty feet away, under the harsh glare of a halogen streetlamp. The occupant sat in the darkened driver's seat. He stared at me, his narrowed eyes tracking my walk all the way from the restaurant, across to the illuminated door of the store. Inside, as I shopped for my cans of stella, I constantly cast a nervous look back in the direction of the door.

I swear I had seen this movie. It's the one where the causal beer buying innocent, gets unceremoniously gunned down by the disgruntled and slightly screw loose railroad employee, who mistakes him for the man who has been dallying with Dixie-Lou from the laundromat.

I bought my beers as quickly as I could and jogged back across the enormous parking lot and into the relative, if confined, safety of my room.

GRAND CANYON

In the morning, I awoke with a long and noisy stretch and surprised myself by touching all four walls, the floor and the ceiling of the room at the same time. I showered quickly and went in search of breakfast. There was a sign pointing to the dining room across the parking lot, but the door was locked and when I asked at reception, they told me that breakfast hadn't been served in almost two years. I pointed out the sign but all I got in return was a shrug and a helmet bereft of crumbs and protein.

I pulled out of the car park and turned left onto Route 66.

I was amped.

For many, it is a much-treasured bucket list thing to do, to ride down the road that once connected the east to the west, the four-thousand miles of road that was once christened '*The Main Street of America.*' In the Grapes of Wrath, Steinbeck named it the '*Mother Road*'. For him, the road symbolised escape and new beginnings.

But the hard truth is that not much of the original road remains. It has largely been slowly replaced by the Interstate system. I was fortunate enough to be able to ride one of the small sections that remains, so avoiding Interstate-40 that would whisk me away to the east. I revelled in taking the slower but infinitely more enjoyable route.

Away from Kingman, the road once again paralleled the railway line. I think that in Kingman, all roads parallel a railway line. For the first hour of the ride, low hills lay off in the far distance, separated from me by the same flat scrubland I had ridden through the day before. But soon, the hills began to rise around me, a series of rolling dusty, gorse speckled hillocks.

Back in the 1930s and 1940s businesses along Route 66 boomed as communities to the east were displaced from the farms and small towns devastated by the dust bowl and subsequent economic crisis. Thousands once travelled this road in pursuit of the golden promise that was California, and their business brought thriving revenue and prosperity to the motels and shops that sprang into sudden existence as they did so.

Now there is very little thriving being done along Route 66. Closed storefronts and garages are sprinkled along it. The only things that remain are the increasingly decrepit historic roadside signs, symbols of something that once was. Something that is sadly, no longer.

The railroad finally left me at a place called Crozier. I had been keeping pace with a diesel cargo train for the last twenty or thirty miles. It was immensely long. I tried to count the trucks but kept getting lost having to pay attention to the road and all, but I think I got up to around forty trucks, all filled with cement and aggregate, bound for somewhere like Phoenix I guessed. The train was strung out across the bigger part of the horizon.

Sometimes the train was close. Close enough for me to the see the driver. I like to think that we shared a nod, an acknowledgment, each cowboy riding his own iron horse across this vast and empty prairie. At other times the tracks separated our paths as the train was pulled out into the desert for several miles.

As the railroad severed our paths for the final time the driver blew his horn. A long and mournful wail to break the solace of the day. Is there any sound so lonesome and sadly evocative as the horn of an American locomotive?

I am pretty sure that the siren blast was for me and me alone. A farewell from one lonely traveller to another. I gave a little wave of acknowledgement to the driver, but I doubt that he saw me as he swung away into the desert to my right and disappeared forever behind a low bluff.

I noticed that the bars on the fuel gauge were down to the last solid block on the display, so pulled off the road to fuel the bike at a small cluster of shanty type dwellings the locals had somewhat hopefully named Peach Springs.

The town was like so many along Route 66, once wildly affluent, but now isolated, poor, and abandoned. A small oasis in the vastness of the desert, slowly being consumed by the creeping sands and encroaching heat. Once fertile, but barren now, left behind by generations of travellers who prefer to be whisked through the landscape on the swift but sterile interstate only a few miles to the south.

On the very edge of town, I was surprised to see a fancy new hotel – The Hualapai Lodge and wondered who on earth could be vacationing in such an out of the way location. Then I saw the row of Harley Davidsons in the parking lot and my question was answered. If you recall, when we were back in Sturgis we already chatted about the 1970s movie '*Easy Rider.*'

Easy Rider was filmed along Route 66. The film was, essentially a very American ode to freedom. The central tenet of the movie contemplated the brittle friction between violence, prostitution, and drugs, all set against a picture postcard scenery of religion and American 'Old Glory' flag waving patriotism.

Harley riders had rediscovered the road and had made it a tourist destination. But the sentimentality that drives modern Harley riders to ride the road today is founded mostly on fragile nostalgia and the desperate need for validation, of the authenticity of something, that had long since slipped away and, in truth, no longer exists.

The day was already hot, and I was hungry and thirsty so at the next town, a place called Seligman I pulled off the road and into the car park of the Roadkill Café. The hand painted sign from the road was of a giant, voracious looking vulture holding a fork, with the words '*You kill it, we grill it,*' printed underneath. I was hooked.

Inside the owners had decorated the place like an old saloon and the menu sported such originally named items such as the '*Splatter Platter,*' the '*Rigor Mortis Tortoise,*' and the '*Bad-Brake Steak.*'

I ordered the special. It was called the '*Guess that Mess,*' and if you could identify the meat in it you got to eat for free. I guessed incorrectly, apparently it was neither Roadrunner or Coyote, so I had to shell out the full $13 dollars. I didn't care. The coke was icy cold, and the air conditioning hummed away until I was refreshed and ready, once more, to hit the road.

Route 66 ended close to the town of Ash Fork where there was no choice but to merge onto the much busier I-40. I passed through Williams and saw the road I would take later to re-join with Paula for the night close to the rim of the Grand Canyon. But first I wanted to tick two more trivial somethings off my odd little American bucket list.

I got to do the first thing about an hour later. At the junction of North Kinsley, and another small but surviving loop of Route 66, is a monument to the Eagles song, Take it Easy. So, I did what I had always wanted to do. I stood on the corner in Winslow Arizona the song had immortalized. Only for about thirty seconds or so you understand. Once I had done it, I realized that it wasn't that special at all. But there is a fetchingly huge Route 66 mural painted at the intersection and a bronze full-size statue of a guy also standing on the corner in Winslow Arizona, so that technically made two sad and lonely middle-aged guys who had made poor choices about the things we wanted to see before we joined the choir eternal and took our final naps in the dirt.

With that small excitement completed, I re-joined I-40 to ride back a few miles so that I could exit south onto a dusty side road that disappeared behind a Marathon fuelling station. The road was narrow. The black tarmac, straight as a die, a ribbon of sun cracked road that led through a veritable Martian landscape. Red dust and low scrub bushes surrounded me as far as the eye could see. The road slowly rose in elevation and then, for no obvious reason, turned in two or three tight sweeping bends, even though there was absolutely nothing to navigate or go around, and I arrived in the inauspicious looking parking lot.

Winslow had been a thrill, but here, I was actually having palpitations.

I walked up the steps to the visitor's centre, paid my entry fee and then stepped out of the chilly air conditioning to stand in awe on the vast rim of Meteor Crater. This was a sight I had wanted to see ever since I had first watched the movie Starman, starring Jeff Bridges. It is the location his alien character must return to, in order to be picked up by his alien buddies.

Meteor Crater is vast. It is 3,900 feet in diameter, and 560 feet deep. A Boeing 737 could almost fit entirely within its circumference. It is surrounded by a rim that rises 148 feet above the surrounding plains and is described as the best-preserved meteorite crater on the planet.

The crater was created in the Pleistocene era, about 50,000 years ago by a nickel-iron meteorite. The meteorite was only 160 feet across, half the length of a football pitch but it had velocity and inertia on its side. It was travelling at a fairly atmosphere incinerating 45,000 miles per hour.

Woolly Mammoths and Giant Ground Sloths would have heard a deep rumble and looked up in confusion at the sky, just in time to see a blaze of light above the land that was yet to be called Arizona. The land might not yet have been granted a name, but this particular spot was just about to be turned into magma.

The energy of the impact has been estimated at ten Megatons of TNT. By comparison, the bomb that flattened Hiroshima was a paltry fifteen Kilotons.

I spent an enjoyable hour or so walking along the rim of the crater and looking at the exhibits in the visitor's centre. They even have a fragment of the meteorite, the Holsinger fragment. It is only two and a half feet across because the bulk of the meteorite would have vaporised on impact. You could easily reach out and hold it in the palms of your hands, like some roughly cylindrical Labrador puppy. But its inky, crystalline black surface exudes mass and heft. It *looks* heavy.

This single, small fragment weighs a whopping one thousand four hundred and nine pounds. It is composed of all sorts of iron, nickel, carbon and silicon carbide.

Time was getting on and I had to be heading out to meet up with my wife again. We had booked a hotel room in the town of Tusayan that services the visitors to the canyon. I had a boring two-hour ride back west and then north but as always, the V-Strom pulled like a fourteen-year-old boy who had just stumbled upon the lingerie pages of the Kay's shopping catalogue.

I happily turned off the busy interstate at Flagstaff and headed north. My heart skipped an actual beat when, for the first time in what felt like a month of only flatness, barren desert, and shimmering heat, I saw through the pine trees the occasional welcoming glimpse of Humphreys Peak, a pleasingly lofty and snow-capped mountain in the distance.

I pulled into the hotel car park and parked the Suzuki around the back close to the staff vehicles and underneath a sodium lamp. Paula was waiting for me in the hotel room, so I hastily showered and changed into a t-shirt less likely to scuttle away on its own and we went back downstairs to go take a look at the Grand Canyon.

Now, I have to be honest. I haven't been everywhere, far from it in fact. But I have been to a fair few places, and it has been my general experience that real-life things and places often fail to live up to the hype that has been generated regarding them. They often fail to live up quite badly.

I think that this is truer in more modern times. Social media, TV travel shows and magazines bombard us with photographs and descriptions using superlative after superlative until our senses become as blunt as a bag of hammers. Very often the angle of the filming or the false perspective forced by the photographer gives a highly unrealistic expectation to the true dimensions, like the shots of the surfers at Nazaré in Portugal, or every photo ever taken by an Estate Agent.

So, I was more than pleasantly surprised to have my flabber thoroughly gasted as I stepped up to the edge of the canyon and looked out across its vastness. The Grand Canyon is large on a scale approaching the universe when viewed through mortal senses. The northern edge of the canyon was hazed by the ten miles that separated it from the rim on which I was standing. Its depth was difficult to discern without leaning outward at such an angle that the small rocks at the edge of my cringing toes began to slip and fall, a very long and sheer mile to the bottom.

Like the Badlands, every millennium of the last two-billion years is written, loud and clear, for all to see in distinct red, grey, and ochre bands of geological activity and slowly settled sediment. The entirety of the canyon is difficult for the human mind to process. It is intricate and colourful, complex, and visually overwhelming. It is far more than a single canyon. The Colorado River has many tributaries, and each has slowly, but inexorably, carved canyons and sub-canyons that make up the whole. If you have the chance to visit and stand on the rim, please do so. It is a gloriously visceral experience.

And so, with my breath suitably taken away we rode back to the hotel. When we got back, there was a show taking place. Some performers from the nearby Havasupai Indian Reservation were entertaining the guests with some tribal singing and dancing, clothed in their ceremonial garbs.

I was conflicted. In some ways the performance was a way for the Havasupai to maintain their identity, their rich culture and history and, at the same time to make a quick buck from the wealthy pale faced tourists. But on the other hand, it felt false to me, performing their arts here, in the lobby of a hotel, on lands stripped from them by the very forefathers of those they sought to entertain.

So, we retired to the bar, and I ordered a lovely cold pint of Stella.

Prescott

Paula had to catch an early flight back to Atlanta, so with her safely in a taxi, I messed around in the expensive hotel room for an hour or so, uncomfortably padding around in a robe that had been previously wrapped around some other blokes body a hundred times and those odd slippers they insist on providing, while I made certain that I had consumed all of the coffee, tea, sugar and creamers.

I had a shower and poured onto myself and scrubbed into the few still hairy parts of me the sudsy contents of all of the tiny bottles of shampoo, conditioner and soap. I put the Gideons Bible, sewing kit and shoe mitt into my tank bag, to sit alongside the three or four other shower caps that I knew, deep down, that I would never, ever again find a use for.

The Gideons Bible I would later place in the fiction section of a public library. It's not much of a hobby but it keeps me busy and entertained.

It was time to start making my slow way back across country to make sure I was back in time to see Ben graduate his 'A' school. 'A' school is short for ascension training, and it is where the new sailors receive vocational type training, so they have the basic knowledge required to be successful in their chosen field of the Navy.

I had promised I would meet Paula back home in Atlanta before riding down to Pensacola, Florida to see him for a day or so on the beach. I would then ride across Florida to Jacksonville, to see him leave on the aircraft carrier to join his new command in Japan.

I packed the Suzuki and did a little maintenance in the back of the hotel, tightening and lubricating the chain and cleaning three inches of dead bug goo off the headlight, indicators, and fairing.

I re-joined the Interstate at Williams and headed east as far as Flagstaff. Traffic was light and it was only an hour later I turned onto I-17 to head south. A few minutes later I turned off the Interstate to cruise down State Road 89A.

This was an even quieter stretch of road that would take me through the heart of Sedona and then onward through some mountainous roads across to Prescott. The first part of the ride was through a straggly and ancient pine forest. It was a beautiful day to be out and about on a fast bike. The V-Strom fairly hummed along. The sky was clear and crisp in the hills as I continued to climb, high distant peaks glimpsed through the trees. I hoped to catch sight of a bear but the woods on either side remained empty.

The road had run in the fairly straight and typically dull American fashion for several miles until I reached a place called Oak Creek when the road suddenly dipped and a tight righthand bend almost took me by surprise. The trees had hidden much of the distant vista but suddenly the skyline opened up to reveal three not so distant peaks with a huge drop off into a wooded valley to my left.

I must have unknowingly gained quite a lot of elevation because now I was losing it at quite an astonishing rate, as the road twisted and turned itself around the peaks to descend into the valley below.

The road had clearly been blasted out of the cliff face to my right. Tumbled rocks still lay piled twenty-feet high, with only a low guard rail protecting me from an even faster descent. On the tight right handers, it felt like my helmet was mere inches from the canyon wall.

The peaks were mostly bald, with just the occasional stand of pine clinging desperately to their rocky edifices. The ribbon of road took a fast and circuitous route around the hills, the Suzuki helping me out with its torquey range and quietly forgiving manners. We swooped around each bend with ease, the visor cracked, enjoying the cool of the hills and the smells of the pine forest.

I approached one really, tight righthander a bit too fast, and my survival reactions kicked in to overrule both my brain and half-forgotten experience. I cogged it down one gear too many and with white knuckles on the throttle I failed to blip the throttle to rev match correctly. The rear tyre gave a happy little chirp and let go. Full credit to the V-Strom, it slid around with both grace and style. Everything was loosey goosey back there for one really, long second and then, without a hint of a high side, it reconnected with the tarmac and propelled me around the bend, the right-hand foot peg making a little scraping sound as it touched down for a millisecond.

I gave out a little whoop of delight, and even pretended, for a moment of two, that I had intended to slide the rear wheel around the bend, Marc Marquez style, and get the pegs down. And then, I immediately backed right off the throttle and rode like my grandmother for the remainder of the descent.

I knew I was getting close to the valley floor when a little bridge swept me across Oak Creek. It was a raging confluence of brown ice water, carrying sediment noisily down from the hills behind me.

In the valley floor I entered the Coconino National Forest, and was, once more, surrounded by a shroud of conifers and then, quite suddenly, a long continuous mountain range was revealed to my right. The sun came in broken shafts of dazzling light through the trees, strobing across my visor in a most photosensitive epilepsy inducing manner.

The mountains were steep. They rose from the valley to reach their summits spectacularly swiftly. At first, they were the colour of white bone, stripped of any hue by the leaching of the sun, but quickly they shifted shades, became dappled with ochre and copper.

In and out of the trees I rode. Sunlight flashed across my eyes and then I would re-enter the darkness of the trees, my retinas struggling to keep pace with the rapid changes of light levels.

I blinked again as the vista opened once more to reveal red and bright orange-rock formations, towering sculptures of sandstone, deep canyons, and colourful buttes. I had arrived in Sedona.

Suddenly, this lad from Southport, England, found himself in the land of all of the cowboy movie films of his youth. The rock sculptures and scenery in the area were used as the backdrop of nearly sixty major Hollywood movie productions of the mid-twentieth century, from 1926 through to the 1970s. '*The Last Wagon*', '*3:10 to Yuma*,' and '*Broken Arrow*' were all filmed there.

The scenery everywhere you looked was spectacular. I had heard of Sedona but hadn't really understood what it represented. The town is quaint, if a little artsy and filled with bijou and wildly expensive studios whose owners tend to be up their own chuffs. But the opportunities for hikes and making breath-taking memories in the countryside around the town is possibly without equal. If Sedona isn't on your bucket list yet, make a note.

I preferred some of the quieter scenery to the south of the town. It was just as coloured by the unique type of sandstone that blesses the geography typical of the area, but the natural architecture created by the constant erosion and weathering, stands apart in more isolated towers of sandstone. Each naturally chiselled sculpture rises from the perfect flat of the valley floor to create individually towering red peaks that reach like crooked fingers into the unspoiled blue of the sky.

Slowly, the red leeched from the rocks, and I was returned once more to a flat, white bleached desert area, sandwiched between the peaks that were now a distant red glow in my rear-view mirrors and the dusty obsidian peaks of the Mingus Mountain that loomed in front of me on the very distant horizon.

As I rode through the Verde Valley, the distant mountain range grew slowly but inexorably as I ploughed my way through the chaparral of scrub, broken rock, and dust until the mountain range finally dominated the skyline, a tall granite edifice that leapt like a kraken from the desert floor.

I stopped on the outskirts of the town of Clarkdale to fill up with gas at the '*#1 Food Store and Sandwich Shop*'.

I filled the Suzuki up with gas and paid at the pump. I was after all in America, and you can pay at the pump there because it's not the third world. I then strolled into the shop to see if there was a bathroom, and to peruse the choice of sandwiches on offer.

There was a toilet for guests located in the back, but a prior patron had generously filled the bowl with his own particularly fragrant blend of bangers and mash. With a gag, I tried to flush, but only succeeded in diluting the mess slightly and breaking the crust that had formed, thus releasing a stench which made me emit a little "hurp," noise. I decided to hold my water as they say.

Back in the shop I mentioned the disaster that was the only toilet in the building to the bored and pimply youth who was pretending to be the store manager. He gave me a look that screamed, 'what the hell do you want me to do about it,' and simply turned his back on me. So, I told him to just fuck his delicious looking sandwiches and stormed off to get back on my bike.

Now both hungry and bursting for a pee I turned my attention back towards the mountain. It appeared, from the floor of the valley, to be an intimidatingly lofty climb. I cinched up the strap on my helmet and resolutely pulled on my gloves like a fighter about to enter the arena.

But upon starting on the climb, it actually turned out to be an easy and delightfully twisty ascent. The road builders had navigated a path that led gently up the mountain through a series of long stretches of road that climbed gradually, punctuated by easy, smooth switchbacks that hauled the Suzuki and me up towards the mountain top, and the small copper mining town of Jerome.

I parked the bike to have a quick look around the town that sits at a lofty elevation of 5,000 feet. Some of the houses were almost Alpine in character, many clinging to the almost sheer cliffs. The rich seams of copper brought wealth to the town in the 1920s when ten-thousand people made it their home. The town nearly failed when the copper ran out and the population dwindled to just one-hundred die hard old timers. Now the town is home to a thriving little population of over four-hundred independent shop owners and artisans.

The town claims to be haunted, and at first blush it does indeed have the look of an old and long abandoned mining town, with its rows of clapboard buildings and abandoned, derelict wagons.

But the shops were doing a solid trade to the few tourists who had been lured away from the yogi retreats and hippy led Jeep tours of nearby Sedona. The shops in Jerome sold all sorts of quirky, fun stuff. Bogus mining paraphernalia, minerals, and crystals. I nearly bought a baseball cap with the words, *"Jerome. Why Am I Here Again?"* emblazoned on the front, but retailing as it did at close to thirty dollars, I found that I didn't have a suitably witty answer to the slogan so put it back on the shelf.

With a stomach still rumbling and a bladder about to split, I waddled into the Haunted Hamburger restaurant. I first paid a hasty visit to the pristine, sparkling bathrooms where I stood up to have a long and noisy wee, and then sat down in the restaurant to eat a cheeseburger.

As I paid, I playfully asked the owner if he really had a ghost. I smiled inanely as the owner told me that he had named the restaurant due to the 'uncanny' disappearance of lots of hammers that belonged to the contractors who were involved in the renovation when he bought the place in 1976.

Back in England we only have 13th century headless coachmen, poltergeists and the Grey Lady who walks the walls of Glamis Castle. In Jerome they have a ghost younger than me that steals hammers. I love America's upbeat and fun interpretation of most things, but haunted houses. I ask you.

The other side of the mountain was a lot of fun. A fifteen-mile ribbon of twists and turns swept me down the south flank of the Mingus Mountain. Fast, gradual turns made the grins stretch wide. The V-Strom was a joy to flick through the bends, the V-Twin thundering through the valleys and powering easily out of each bend until I reached, once more, the floor of the valley.

Arizona was becoming a blast. One of my favourite states to ride through. The topology changed constantly. High arid plains, punctuated by cool craggy mountains, and now I was riding down a road that replicated my personal definition of what I always thought of as America.

I was on a dead straight road. The landscape beside me was one of flat waving grass. A prairie. In front, in the distance, was a small and ancient pick-up truck. As I got closer, I could see it was an old 1940s baby blue Chevrolet. It looked like it had been used every day since it rolled off the production line in Detroit. Hauling feed from the merchant and livestock to market. In the back was a big old farm dog of questionable pedigree and when I drew level, I thought the same could be said of the driver. He was older than the truck and had skin burnished copper and wrinkled by ten thousand suns. He gave me a friendly wave from beneath his battered white Stetson as I gunned the Suzuki to pass him.

The sun was lowering in the sky when I pulled into the town of Prescott and parked the bike outside the hotel I had booked. Prescott was, in its day, a true western town. It is packed with history. It was once the capital city of Arizona and was a gold and silver frontier mining town. Both Doc Holliday and Virgil Earp (brother of Wyatt Earp) of the gunfight at the O.K. corral fame lived there. Local conflicts with the Apache were common and the town still hosts the world's oldest rodeo and has done since 1888.

The hotel I was stopping at was also steeped in history. It had been converted by the current owners from what they delicately termed a bordello, into a small hotel. Each of the rooms had clearly belonged to one of the working girls. Each had a small sink (for the washing of bits) and a separate bathroom. A clever little lever could be operated from within the room, to raise a flag outside, to let the next customer know that the lady within was daintily refreshed and ready for the next dusty, horny cowpoke.

After a walk into town for another steak dinner and several cold beers, I returned to the best little whorehouse in Arizona and jumped gleefully into my bed. I began to nod off wondering if Doc Holliday or Wyatt Earp had ever been in this bed for any particularly jiggly reason. As heavy eyelids closed across gritty, tired eyes, I reckoned I was a faster shot than either of them. At least in the bedroom department.

Tucson

I awoke in my cosy hotel room with a long sigh. I had taken too long already to get to where I was. Unfortunately, I had only completed a very small part of the trip back east that I still needed to complete to get back home to Atlanta.

I showered, picked out the least stiff pair of underpants from my little festering tank bag and went down to eat some breakfast. I had to concede, as I sipped my morning coffee and ate the sweet muffin that American's strangely consider to be a breakfast item, that I could have completed the trip across to Prescott much more quickly. I had dillied and dallied as the song goes. With breakfast finished, and an eye on the waitress's back, I quickly filled my helmet for later.

I had stopped in the middle of a desert to look at what I thought to be a totem pole only to find out that it was in fact just a pole. I had taken a detour to find a very unremarkable dam, stopped in what purported to be a little bit of England only to confirm what I already knew — that it wasn't, and even ridden quite a long way to look at a significantly huge hole in the ground.

My ride from Los Angeles had zigged and zagged across parts of what had once been the wild west. It had taken me four days to cover close to twelve-hundred miles. But it was trivial compared to the distance remaining between me and home. I would have to cross all of New Mexico, Texas, and Louisiana —nearly an additional two-thousand miles of riding, some of it through spectacular scenery, but quite a lot through Texas as well.

With the bike packed and ready, I slung a weary leg over the seat and said farewell to Prescott. As I rode back through the pretty town I mused on my journey through a small part of the west. I am certain that my American readers will be screaming at the screen (or pages) telling me that I missed all of the best bits, Yellowstone, The Teton Mountain Range, Monument Valley, and Yosemite.

But I think that has always been a big part of my trips. I have never been as drawn to the Mona Lisa's of this world as much as the undiscovered gems that the locals know are out there, but simply don't get the recognition. There are a thousand documentaries about America's national parks, and I am certain another British TV chef will soon be renting a Harley, to be followed around by a large crew of cameramen, sound technicians, producers, best boys and dolly grips, to make another of the bastard things.

But I ask you. Has Gordon Ramsay, or that fellow who likes butter so much, have they ever taken you to Kingman? On that note, I shall let the jury retire…

I swung the Suzuki south onto State Road 69. The day was picture perfect. A clear blue sky dotted with clouds that could have been drawn by the illustrators of The Simpsons. Traffic was busy on the highway for the first few miles, until I finally managed to leave the usual urban clutter behind me. As the Lowes and Home Depots, Walmart's, McDonalds', and In-N-Out Burgers vanished over the horizon in my mirrors, the traffic dwindled away to leave me mostly alone in a land of rolling hills punctuated by scrubby green bushes.

After thirty minutes of riding, I was forced to join I-17. The scenery remained the same, but as I slowly lost elevation, the temperature once again began to soar.

Close to the town of Anthem, the hills faded away, replaced by a broad and mostly flat desert area. And that's when I saw my first Saguaro Cactus. It stood eight feet tall, completely alone in the desert with its thick, prickly arms raised to the sky in a mock surrender. It made me smile broadly inside my sweaty helmet.

It is funny what few things ended up defining the quintessential essence of America for a lad from the UK. A colleague at work asked me to list them out once. I think he thought I would say something like bald eagles, freedom, and school shootings. But for me it will always be the sight of fireflies and the sound of bullfrogs on a sweltering summer evening just as the light begins to leach from the sky. It is the blast of a distant train blowing its lonesome whistle, and a pale green saguaro cactus standing alone in the shimmering heat haze of a caramel-coloured southwestern desert.

I turned off the highway and rode through the sweltering streets of Phoenix's more affluent suburbs. It was already 114 degrees Fahrenheit, and the streets were mostly deserted. I did see the occasional highly motivated shopper jumping between the pools of shade that the shop canopies afforded, shrinking from the faintest touch of the sun like a vampire caught, returning to his castle late from a night-time of virginal artery bothering, but the shoppers were few and far between.

Inside my helmet the sun blazed down. If somebody had been riding pillion behind me, with a blowtorch against the top of my helmet it couldn't have been any hotter.

I suddenly realized I had no idea where I was and pulled over. A minute later I was stood by the side of the bike, panting, while the Phoenix sun beat down like Cosy Powell on the top of my hairless bonce, wondering what to do and where to go next.

Phoenix, and its sprawling suburb, is a very modern city. Until the 1950s it was a small centre for local agriculture. The area is known as the valley of the sun. It experiences very high daily temperatures and long, sweat filled summers. Phoenix residents will tell you that the heat there is a dry heat and that it really isn't so bad. They are liars. The summers in Phoenix are abhorrent. It can already be in the low hundreds Fahrenheit by the time the sun peeps above the trees.

The real reason Phoenix is a modern city is that before the 1950s, air conditioning did not exist. It took that invention, and the interest of a spattering of high technology companies, lured by low business rates, to move into the area. There was more new construction in Phoenix in 1959 alone than from the previous thirty-two years combined.

I slowly figured out, mainly from the street and shop signs that I was in Scottsdale. Scottsdale is the upmarket part of the suburbs, filled with golf courses, expensive shopping, and artisan fairs. Handsome couples scuttled by, dressed in shorts and loafers that had those little tassels attached, and all decked out in colourful designer wear. All around me were storefronts that bore the logos of Louis Vitton, Prada, and Versace. Each had a store with intimidatingly few garments on view and even more intimidating shop assistants stood by. They stared at me as I walked by, just daring me to walk into their shop with my empty wallet and the dust of the road that perennially hung around me like a filthy and dangerously unhealthy aura.

Afraid that my scalp might spontaneously ignite if I stood out in the sun for much longer, I found a coffee shop to escape the harmful rays and regain my bearings.

Inside was rendered so cold by the aggressive and madly thrumming air conditioning units that I had to put my riding jacket back on. While I stood scratching my head and pondering whether the 'Venti Pumpkin Spice Latte', or the 'Grande Iced Caramel Macchiato' would be more like the plain white coffee I actually craved, I carefully unfolded my large paper map across one of the tables by the windows. This simple action elicited quite a few perplexed and amused glances, as well as a few barely concealed gasps, from the large group of tidy, full-bearded hipster type customers that were frequenting the establishment.

I garnered the kind of rapt attention a time traveller from the past might have attracted. It was as if I had stepped through a portal carrying a cutlas, with a scarlet macaw on one shoulder and one eye concealed by a patch, to unroll a faded yellow treasure map from beneath one arm.

I suspected this crowd had never heard of Rand McNally, Michelin or, my personal favourite, Ordinance Survey. I cared not a jot. Maps are beautiful things and when the skill to navigate by them is finally laid out on the sacrificial altar by Elon Musk or the next Steve Jobs, not only will the world be a much poorer place, but I suspect we, as a species, will be no more.

As my fingernail hovered over Phoenix, I glanced across the map to initially not find my goal of Atlanta at all. I had to unfold two more creases of pages, revealing an expanse of distance that, for a moment, took my breath away.

The challenge I had created for myself was that I needed to be back in Atlanta in only five days' time. I was still 1,800 miles away, a long ride across three states, one of them being Texas which was rather famous for both its heft and considerable width.

I always did this to myself. I had pottered my way around the west and the southwest, taking my own sweet time. It was, after all, full of the bits I wanted to see. But 'past' me had certainly shafted present and future me fairly hard in the arse region. Because now I faced the penalty for all of that goofing around. In front of me I had several long and tedious blasts across all the middle bits of America I wasn't entirely thrilled to see.

My map showed the shortest and fastest route lay to the south. A trawl through south-eastern Arizona and then on through New Mexico before hitting the expanse of Texas and then Louisiana, before crossing back into Mississippi, onward to Alabama and, finally home to Georgia.

I looked at the clock on the wall. Three o'clock in the afternoon. I still had a few hours of daylight left so I walked up to the counter to buy a sandwich and some water to take with me. Not a single pig-based product was on offer, so I ordered a gluten free smashed 'avo' on rye to go and two bottles of still water that cost me nothing short of twenty dollars. I left as quickly as I was able, before my limited amount of facial hair curled up into an unwanted handlebar moustache, and I forgot how to wire a plug or change a flat tyre on a car.

On the hot ride out of Phoenix I passed the Sky Harbor Airport and glanced across with more than a gut wrench of homesickness. The road ahead of me seemed unconquerable. The distances daunting. But I reminded myself that I had done this before. Many times, when I was much younger, and even more foolish. The trick, I seemed to remember from a memory bank both dusty and hazed by the combination of too many years and too many beers, is simply to begin. To begin and then to just to keep on riding, pointing the front wheel at the distant horizon and to keep dreaming of a warm bed and a cold pint at the end of another long day.

I took I-10 to escape the madness of the city streets and was soon travelling through the same arid flatlands that I had ridden into the sprawling city on. The land was almost without feature. The horizon in every direction stretched to the edge of the earth, its uniformity spoiled now and again by a scrub of stunted green bushes or a distant, craggy hillock.

I was tired when I hit the first of the suburbs north of Tucson. The day had been too long and too hot. I pulled into the car park of the first hotel I saw. It was a dismal looking Motel 6 on a strip of land dominated by several other dismal looking buildings. It was an ugly little island of desperate, budget hotels, surrounded on all sides by the never-ending roar of the heavy traffic on the highway.

I had noticed a Waffle House on the ride in. I was so tired and desperate I walked across to it as soon as I had locked the bike and dumped my stuff. The neighbourhood was rough looking, down at heel, filled with litter and broken down and abandoned cars. A group of guys watched me walk across from the hotel. They were dressed in grey hoodies and hidden eyes tracked my progress.

I hoped that the Waffle House waitresses were better armed than the local citizenry. And, knowing Waffle House like I do, I was pretty sure that they would be, and tonight would not be the night I got gunned down over a plate of pancakes.

Mexico

I packed my bags in the room of the Motel 6 and walked down to reception to steal food for lunch. The Suzuki was still parked around back, close to the cars of the employees, where the friendly receptionist had assured me, it would be safe and protected by CCTV.

A desert windstorm must have blown in during the night. The bike was covered in a silvery grey shroud of fine sand. I didn't have time to wash the bike clean, but I was surprised as when I started off down the road, the already warm wind just swept the bike clean, so tiny were the grains. I must have left a silvery cloak of particles in the air behind me.

I had no real alternative but to ride the freeway. Interstate 10 was the only road that etched a thin line of tarmac across the desert and in the general direction I needed to go. I admit to being somewhat despondent that bright morning. The scenery refused to vary from the same beige tapestry I had ridden through for the previous two days.

As soon as I cleared the busy environs of Tucson and the repetitive signs for the airport, I stopped to fill up with gas at a brand-new Triple T Truck Stop. While I was there, I made use of the free air to check the tire pressures. In the distance was the Saguaro National Park and behind that the distant peak of the Mica Mountain range which still bore a silver wig of snow upon its crenulated crown.

Outside the small town of Willcox I pulled off the road to drink some water. The heat had continued to rise as I had ridden, and I was already hot and dehydrated. The air rippled as the baking heat of the sun was reflected back from the blacktop. It turned every distant vista into a blurred and constantly flickering movie scene. I shielded my eyes and could just make out, on the horizon, the two granite peaks of the Dos Cabezas mountain. The two peaks rise from the shoulders of the range like the two heads looking at each other that give the mountain its Spanish name.

The sky was the clearest periwinkle I believe I have ever seen. I almost prayed to a God I didn't believe in for a hint of a cloud and a little spot of rain. But the horizons remained clear, the sun beating down on the stunted and sparse scrubby bushes and parched yellow grasses.

A huge billboard in the middle of absolutely nowhere informed me that I had entered into New Mexico. The billboard also informed that I had entered the *'land of enchantment.'* A bold claim I thought. But based on what reason, was not immediately made clear to me, as I continued to ride through a giant child's sand pit.

The state motto of New Mexico is the slightly puzzling *'It Grows as it Goes,'* which reminded me more of a hopeful erection than something a southern state would aspire to

The scrubland continued and the distant line of low hills that had kept me company all morning continued to lurk on the horizon. If anything, the landscape slowly morphed into something even less enchanting, as at the town of Steins, the mountain slipped away to be replaced by a vast flat, dust bowl of sand that stretched out in front of me for mile after empty and soul-destroying mile.

I pulled off the road at a town called Lordsburg. It was located in the dead centre of bumfuck. I filled up with gas and then walked into the Saucedo's Supermarket to revel in the air conditioning. I stood under a vent for a good five minutes, jacket open, panting heavily like an overworked Labrador, face up to the blast of frigid refreshment. My inactivity finally prompted the cashier to shout across and ask me if I was OK. I responded that I was, and then walked slowly around the aisles to stock up on water and supplies.

Back on the bike I had a slow trundle around the town. The streets were all well paved and ridiculously wide, but the houses were small and mostly derelict. Rumour has it that Billy the Kid used to wash dishes at one the hotels in town during his teenage years. It certainly made sense to me now why, in later life, he left this town to become an outlaw and went on to kill twenty men before being fatally shot himself at the age of only twenty-one.

All that long afternoon I rode through a featureless Venusian landscape, marked only by the passing of the telegraph poles that would have once been the only thing that connected these widely separated townships from anything close to civilization. Before the railroads arrived of course.

The railroad ran alongside me as well, although all through the day not a single train passed me in either direction.

It was late in the afternoon before my sight was finally jolted back into recognition mode by the distant line of hills, that lay like a crumpled piece of paper on the very distant and haze flickered horizon.

I had almost reached the Rio Grande and the town of Los Cruces which sits beneath the Organ Mountains.

I knew I was about to be re-immersed in civilization as, after all of the emptiness of the desert I began to pass signs for the usual scatter of small independent American businesses that always lie along the sides of roads like this, scratching out a living like chicken in a dusty pen. You will find them all across the country, in every rural backwater and sleepy one-horse town. Places that I rode past now, like 'Fair Acres Body Shop Repair,' and 'Torres Welding,' scattered like dice amongst the plethora of corporate Public Self-Storage units, Walmart's and Cracker Barrel outlets.

I crossed the Rio Grande just outside town. The river channel was broad but the river itself was a dirty trickle that formed vast puddles as it wound its slow way south towards the gulf.

Despite being the second most populous city in New Mexico, Las Cruces soon petered out and I was back, heading now almost due south. I was following the river course of the Rio Grande, all the way towards El Paso where I would, once again, pick up the border with nearby Mexico.

Twenty miles or so later I left the Land of Enchantment behind me. I had only seen a little of New Mexico, but I still felt like the moniker to be quite the stretch for a state that simply appeared to have been little more than a giant, baking hot sandcastle kicked over and squashed flat by a petulant child.

If there was a roadside sign that welcomed me into Texas, I missed it. But I instantly knew that I was in Texas by the size of the gargantuan spread of the RV and Camping store that lay on one side of the road and the smoke that poured from the stack of the 'Great American Steakhouse' on the other, both separated by the wide ribbon of tarmac and the single largest American flag I have ever seen. Old Glory waved slowly in the rising heat of the day. Surely a clear message to those unfortunate enough to have been born on the wrong side of the nearby border, that this here land was God's land and that, despite the state motto being 'friendship' the folks around here all carried guns, and foreigners and immigrants were not necessarily included in the sentiment.

Neither the landscape nor the temperature offered much respite, but the proximity to the Rio Grande meant that small ribbons of townships now rode alongside me all the way through the desert until I reached El Paso itself.

I did my best to avoid the tangled, busy sprawl of the city. El Paso sits right along the border with Mexico. On a casual glance at a map, you would see only a single, large and interconnected city. But on closer inspection you would see that the Rio Grande cuts its way through the heart of two very different cities.

On the northern side of the river sits the United States of America and El Paso. On the southern bank is the Mexican city of Cuidad Juárez. Together geographically, but politically forever divided, the two cities still form the largest bilingual and binational workforce in the western hemisphere.

I passed through El Paso and, finally wearied by the relentless heat and interminable dust of the day, I turned off the highway and rode slowly through the mostly deserted street of the border town of Pendale. I had consulted my map, and I was pretty sure that here I would be able to get a glimpse of the famous border wall that Trump had bragged that he would build, and that Mexico would pay for.

The town was neat and tidy with small single-story dwellings with tidy stone filled yards protected by steel mesh bars and railings. The streets wound around, and I got lost a few times and ended up in a cul-de-sac or three.

I finally came out from under a fly-over on Padres Drive and there it was. The road just ended, and in front of me was the border wall. It was thirty-feet high and made of steel construction and designed to be impenetrable. Trump finally managed to build and repair a decent five-hundred miles of border, although it was clear that Mexico would never pay a single peseta to secure another countries border. Five hundred miles is a decent amount, but the total length of the continental border is at least four times the length of the current barrier, the rest being secured by a combination of the Rio Grande itself and modern electronic surveillance technology.

The 'Trump Wall' itself also proved to be far from impenetrable. Over three-thousand breaches have been made since it was constructed, some sections simply being cut open with angle grinders and other power tools.

It was strange to see such a thing up close. Such a physical barrier to keep one countries citizen from another's. I am not going to argue the pros and cons of any countries immigration policies but, in Europe, nothing like it has been seen since the building of Hadrian's Wall that failed to keep the Scots out of England and the notorious Berlin Wall of post war Germany. And we all know how that ended.

I rode back south, through other small border towns, and then, finally, into the car park of a motel in the town of Tornillo which sits, just like El Paso right on the Mexican border.

With a sand filled cough of exasperation, I turned off the engine and just sat still for a moment on the bike listening to both mine and the bike's rattling exhalations as the engine slowly cooled. My head was throbbing. I was desperately hot and hungry at the same time.

The motel in front of me was called the Deluxe Inn and I have to say that having had a day of bold claims proved false, my hopes were low. The motel had the usual row of single floor cabins, all interconnected under an old green shingle roof. The car park was framed by the border wall itself, and was large enough to accommodate a state fare, but only three or four other cars were parked, close to the doors of the owner's dwellings.

I got my key in exchange for a very reasonable fifty-six dollars and opened the door expecting a rush of insectile limbs to scuttle from the light, but the room was small and clean and thankfully free of the usual pests that come for free at such a price.

The shower was basic and rattled and clunked reassuringly when the faucet was turned. But hot water ran clear and free, and the towels were white, although so well worn and threadbare that when I held one up to the window, I swear I could see somebody in a sombrero waving at me through it on the far side of the car park.

On the whole I was very content. Down the road was a little Mexican restaurant called El Jinete, and being within a castanets throw of the country itself, I strode down there now, kicking up the dust like a gunslinger, with my motorcycle induced swagger to order several large beers and some Mexican food.

Seated at a greasy little table I ordered a beer. It arrived in a glass so large and heavy that I was forced to hold it like a little boy, cupped in two hand to tip the icy, frothy contents down my dry throat. With the glass raised to my lips my head completely disappeared behind the rim.

I ordered the special off the extensive menu. It was called 'El Super Combo' and was described as consisting of a burrito, an enchilada and a Chile relleno. I ordered another beer while I waited for the food to arrive. This was the famous 'Tex Mex,' the fusion of the culinary creations of the Tejano people and the state of Texas that I had been told about and had hotly anticipated.

But when it arrived, the food made me deeply sad. The burrito looked and tasted just like the enchilada and the Chile relleno tasted like everything else. It all swam around the plate in a gloop of green, gelatinous salsa Verde that looked and tasted like something a snail might leave behind. I couldn't finish it and pushed the plate away in disgust.

The charming waitress saw me sit back in my chair and with a worried expression, she came over to ask if everything was to my liking. I began to form a complaint in my mind, but my English brain stepped in to take control of this potentially awkward situation.

"It was lovely thanks. Just the check please."

GERMANY?

The next morning, I rolled out of the small bed and staggered across to the shower. I had slept well. On the walk back from the café, I had been pleasantly surprised to have had all of my senses tingled simultaneously by the proximity of another country.

The American town of Tornillo had fallen dark and silent. The occasional window of a house flickered with the light of a television but otherwise the streets were mostly empty. In contrast, on the other side of the Rio Grande, lay the town of Guadalupe that sits inside the vast county of Chihuahua. I was delighted to see that across the river, the lights of Mexico danced and twinkled in the warm evening air. Twanging guitars and voices could be heard as the partygoers sang, and the aroma of the sizzling mix of fajitas and coriander was carried to me on the breeze.

Say what you want to about Mexicans, but only a few hundred yards away, there was a fiesta going down, and they were all having a damn sight better time than the sleepy residents of Tornillo had ever had.

The day was very young when I packed the bike, the sun barely grazing the low roofs of the Motel. On the other side of the river the fiesta had ended and only silence stretched itself across the small distance that kept us apart.

Today my goal was Austin, an ambitious five hundred plus miles ride across the great expanse of this massive state. I suspected, even before I swung my leg over the bike and fired up the engine that I was to fall short of the day's target. But I intended to make as much of the ride as I could to shorten the last few days ride back to Atlanta and home.

The road initially took me south along the course of the Rio Grande. The names of the small towns so American on one side of the river, Fort Hancock and Clint. And so Spanish and much more romantic sounding and filled with both mystery and history on the other, San José de Paredes and Rinconada de Gallegos.

At the town of Esperanza, the road preformed a dog leg kick away from the river and never returned. The road took me almost due east, past the heat and wind crumbled peaks of the Quitman Mountains.

The terrain remained desert but was filled now with some scant greenery and an increasing sign of life. Hardy desert olives, creosote bushes, cool green yucca and spiky yellow agarito lined the culverts and any of the shade filled divots scattered across the landscape.

The day wore long as I travelled eastward on roads that were straight and without end. A single ribbon of tarmac that was drawn from the front imprint of my tyre all the way, in one continuous, bold sharpie line, to touch with a smudge on the very distant horizon.

I tried to keep myself active and engaged on the bike. I knew that the desert here was home to mountain lions, coyotes, armadillos, and antelope. As I rode, I scoured the hills and buttes for signs of life but, to my disappointment, I saw nothing.

I rode through the tiny towns of Allamore and Van Horn. Small settlements eking out an existence in the midst of not very much else at all. Tired looking towns built of corrugated steel, RV's and despair. Jeff Bezos is rumoured to own a ranch to the north of Van Horn, but you wouldn't know it. The small houses sat on neat, well-tended lots, each with at least two pickup trucks up the drives. But the towns lacked identity. All at sea in a literal desert. Other than the accident of birth, I had to wonder what else brings you to, and subsequently leaves you in such a place.

The day continued to wear on. The unrelenting, suffocating heat and barrenness of the surrounding wilderness continued to drive me bat shit crazy with boredom, although the Suzuki seemed not to care a whit about where or how we rode. The bike just continued to buzz away underneath me, pulling strongly and riding steadily throughout the day, and returning a solid fifty miles per gallon through the long day as it did so.

I pulled off the interstate at Ozona to rest, to find somewhere with air conditioning and a bathroom and to get a bite to eat. I had the Double X hamburger at the Hitchin Post Steakhouse, seated in a little booth and bathed in the literal cool of the air conditioning.

I was hot and sweaty, and despite having taken a shower only that morning, my armpits insisted on competing with the grilled meat to be crowned the gamiest thing in Texas. I was forced to clamp my arms down to my side to stifle the rising miasma, whenever the pretty waitress came by to fill up, once again, my tall, ice-beaded glass of water.

Back on the road, and at least feeling full and somewhat refreshed I continued to press on eastwards. Habitations dwindled and the number of towns became more and more sparse. After I left Ozona a full forty-five minutes passed before I rode past the equally small town of Sonora, with absolutely nothing in between them. Not a single gas station, residence, warehouse, farmhouse, henhouse, outhouse or doghouse.

Texas is huge. It is famously the second largest state in the Union, beaten only by Alaska. But like Alaska, outside of the few major cities, the state is largely empty. Texas is nearly three times as large as the United Kingdom. Both France and Spain are smaller than Texas. But the difference in Europe, is that our ancient and well lived in countries, are positively riddled with hamlets, villages, towns, and cities. I admit that the interior of Spain can sometimes feel a tad rural and desolate, but it has absolutely nothing on Texas, and of course the food in Spain is immeasurably better and more varied. And to add significant insult to injury, Spain even has sombreros, donkeys, decent healthcare, and Benidorm.

It was soon after I passed the town of Sonora that the landscape finally began to change. The shift was very subtle at first. It was like somebody was slowly turning up the green colour contrast control on an old television set. Slowly, the mostly empty scrub of the western desert retreated and the fields on either side of me began to fill with softly waving grass and the occasional twisted Mesquite Tree.

By the time I got to Segovia I could have been riding through Welsh Wales. Well, not quite, but the landscape had certainly become lusher. Texas Red Oaks and Pecans lined the road, and the fields were rolling and cultivated. I even saw some signs for a winery although, as much as I peered into the fields, I didn't see a single vine.

As I approached the town of Fredericksburg, I checked both my map and my state of mind. The map told me I was still close to two hours away from Austin and my mind was waving a little white flag of surrender and telling me that I was toast.

I was cooked, broiled, overheated and so severely under stimulated that I was close to slipping into a catatonic coma. I needed to stop riding for the day. I had never heard of Fredericksburg, but my map showed that it was the only decent sized town, for literally miles in any direction, I pulled off the interstate and started to look for a place to stay that was both cheap and certain to disappoint.

For a moment or two I was sure that the combination of the intense boredom of riding through western Texas and the punishing heat had brought on a small stroke.

I seemed to, all of a sudden, be riding through a small town in rural Germany. The hotels and motels all had Teutonic names such as '*The Hoffman Haus*.' '*Hotel Kitsmiller*,' and '*The Dietzel Motel*.'

The boutique shops, restaurants and bars were all similarly named, "*Otto's Bistro*' lay alongside '*Marketplatz von Frederickburg*.'

As I rode, all tourist signs pointed me towards the '*Pioneer Museum*,' so I parked the bike on the broad and handsome main street and walked inside to steal the air conditioning and see if there were any free snacks to be had.

Well, what a strange little story awaited me in this rural backwater of Texas. The museum told the tale of a population in Germany, in the mid-nineteenth century, that was increasingly unhappy with its own ruling government. At the same time, Texas was desperately in need of citizens to help populate the state and to help keep the Mexican army at bay. The German revolutionists, most of whom were highly educated, were excited at the thought of a new life under the newly formed US Constitution. The Germany government was equally glad to see these troublemakers go and organised over forty-five ships to carry twelve-thousands of its own citizens all the way across the Atlantic to Texas.

The first group of German settlers reached the Pedernales Valley and the location between the Town Creek and

Baron's Creek surrounded by seven hills on May 8, 1846, and called their new town Fredericksburg. A little piece of Germany was firmly established in the heart of Texas. German was still the predominant language in the town until the 1940s.

Isn't America great for that sort of story. Its full of unexpected microcosms of culture and life. It is a country founded and established by immigrants. Without them it could never have become the country it is today.

Today, the town is still very popular with German tourists and hotel prices were ridiculously expensive. I was forced far outside of town to find somewhere cheap enough to stay. But first I sat down at the Auslander Restaurant on Main Street and ate a huge plate full of Käsewurst, a spicy sausage served with sauerkraut, all washed down with a stein of cold German pilsner.

GALVESTON

The motel I ended up in was both cheap and disappointing in equal amounts. It was so far out of town that I may as well have carried on riding to Austin. But with a full stomach and the benefit of one or two pilsners I had slept well.

I found some breakfast in the lobby. As well as the strange foodstuffs American's consume in the morning such as sweet muffins and far too fluffy pancakes, the motel had laid on a more continental offering, so my helmet was soon smelling of garlic sausage and spicy salami.

While I sipped my coffee, I poured over my Rand McNally Road map. Here in rural Texas the sight of a paper map didn't elicit the same response as it had done with the hipsters of Scottsdale Arizona.

I pondered for quite a while the relative merits of two alternative routes I might take. One lay directly to Austin. I had originally planned on this route as it would allow me to go and see for myself the relatively new Circuit of the Americas racetrack. There was no race taking place, I just wanted to go see it.

Stupid I know. But it was a personal vanity ride. I had long planned on visiting the circuit with an old friend of mine, so that we could watch Rossi together, to see our mutual hero ride, and possibly win, a MotoGP there. We had talked about it constantly. This year, but if not this year, definitely the next.

But then our plan was permanently iced. My old friend, only forty-seven years old passed away unexpectedly before we could put our plan into action. Rossi retired in the same season.

I really wanted to go see the circuit, but if I took that route, the sensible way back to Atlanta would take me north, firstly to Dallas and then inland, across more tedious country.

The alternative route was slightly longer, but would take me to the coast, firstly to Galveston on the Gulf of Mexico, and then across to New Orleans, before being forced back inland to cross Mississippi and Alabama.

I folded my map with a rustle of resolution. The coast it would be. If I ever visited the Circuit of the Americas, it would be like any normal, sensible biker would do. When there was a bloody race to watch!

I took State Road 290 out of town and immediately started to see the vines of the wineries in the fields on either side. I crossed the bright twinkle of the Pedernales River and then turned right onto the single lane road labelled 1376, and I knew instantly that I had made the right decision to ride to Galveston. I was back on country roads, away from the bustle of the interstate. I was smiling and happy as I cogged the V-Strom down a gear and rolled the throttle all the way back.

The roads were twisty and smooth and the sun, as always, shone from an azure sky. The fields were filled with meadow flowers. Tall trees painted the horizon a sculpted mosaic of tangled branches. Amazing how the simple smell and sight of grass and trees can fill the senses. I drank it all in, expelling the dust of the southwest from my lungs and replacing it with the sweet and heady draught of an insect filled summer.

After an hour of riding, I found a little parking place by the side of Snake Creek. I parked the bike and sat down close to the babbling creek to drink a bottle of water. After the overheated slog of the previous day, this morning was perfect. The roads were empty and, even though the weather was still hot, being immersed in greenery and listening to the sound of the nearby river made both my little water break, and the ride so far, enjoyable.

I have always had a gift of being able to, in an otherwise empty field, lay the picnic blanket out on the angry ant's nest, or to pitch a tent on top of the only hornets in a five-mile radius. Today my gift extended to venomous snakes. I had just finished my bottle of water and was starting to walk back through the long grass back to the bike when I nearly stepped on a large water moccasin that was warming itself on the hot ground.

Luckily, I had grown used to snakes having lived in the south-eastern United States for over fifteen years and, like a Ray Mears or a Steve Irwin, I knew exactly how to handle this potentially tricky and dangerous encounter. I let out a shriek so high pitched it made a nearby dog start to howl and, mid-step, with only one foot on the ground, still somehow manage to leap six feet into the air.

My manly yell scared the snake and it slivered thickly away into the undergrowth by the riverbank. With us both suitably startled and with adrenalin now spurting from my nose and ears I fanned a hand in front of my face to get some air and muttered a breathless, "Well, I do declare…"

and hurried back to the bike and set off back on my journey.

At least now I knew why the locals had given the creek its name.

I continued the ride south and east, on my little backroads, avoiding I-10 that would whisk me towards busy Houston. I took State Road 183 to the sweet little town of Gonzalez where I stopped to eat my pilfered lunch in the green and pleasant Kerr Creek Park. Opposite the park was Gary's Gun Repair store and the First Shot Liquor store. Guns and hard liquor, has there ever been a better pairing?

Texas has very few gun laws. Open carry without a permit was once more made legal in 2021 and it's not unusual to see folks just walking around with holstered pistols or even AR type weapons. That can be said of much of the United States of course, but Texas and by association, Texans, seem to have a special affinity for the second amendment. Texas is always the one state that threatens to want to secede from the rest of the Union. In the 1990s, Texas began to use the slogan "Texas. It's Like a Whole Other Country."

When you hear politicians say that kind of thing out loud, you should believe them. Word for word. There are still folks out there who would prefer that Texas once more resorts to being the independent republic it was before it became the twenty-eighth state on December 29th, 1845. I honestly don't have a view either way on the rights or wrong of such a position, but it is genuinely strange to hear dissention to such a degree anywhere else in a United Sates that is otherwise so loyal to the flag.

I took State Road 90 almost due east. The gravity well pull of Houston was unavoidable. Like all large cities, all the roads lead there eventually but, for the moment, I was still enjoying the ride through that flat, green, and pleasant horse country.

It was on the other side of Rosenberg, as I crossed the Brazos River, that the inevitable busy suburbs and environs of Houston made their presence known. As if by magic all of the AutoZones, Captain Ds, CVS, McDonalds and Walmart's sprang from the ground to surround me in their retail ugly embrace. Gigantic billboards filled the sky and overhead power cables strung from pylons competed with the myriad American flags that flew from every other outlet.

All of what were surely once small quaint towns had slowly, over the passing of years and rezoning permits, and the pouring of an obscene amount of concrete, they had slowly but inexorably merged into one large urban mass. At a place called Sugar Lands I turned off onto State Road 6 to head south in an attempt to keep the city at bay. It looked like a country road on my map but still turned out to be a busy four-lane carriageway.

Palm trees sprang up to replace the tall oaks and then I found myself suspended above the grey of the Gulf Coast on the Galveston Causeway that whisked me the short distance across to Galveston Island and then onward to the town of Galveston itself.

Galveston had long been one of those places I had yearned to see. Galveston beach is still rather pretty, if constrained by the busy outlet lined highway that runs its length, and the constant rumble of traffic that thunders along it.

You might be thinking that I wanted to visit Galveston because I am a huge Glen Campbell fan. I am obviously. Who isn't. But the real reason I wanted to see it for myself was because a few years before my visit I had read a book called, '*Isaac's Storm.*'

The book was written by the very talented Erik Larson and tells the tale of the almost total destruction of Galveston. Larson tells the tale in a non-fiction novelistic style and centres the story around a local meteorologist, our protagonist, Isaac Cline.

In the story, despite all evidence to the contrary, Isaac senses that a greats storm is brewing in the warm waters of the Gulf. He predicts a humongous hurricane, one with the power to destroy a coastal town such as the one he is living in. But nobody will listen to him, and no action is taken to evacuate. The hurricane lands, as Isaac has predicted, at nightfall on September 7th, 1900.

The category four hurricane makes landfall, bringing one-hundred and twenty mile an hour sustained winds and a deadly sixteen-foot storm surge. On the mainland the monitoring stations realise that Galveston has fallen eerily silent.

On the island, the waters rise quickly and soon the entire island is destroyed, washed away by the ferocity of the wind and the quickly rising waters. Ten thousand people died that night as houses were first flooded and then completely washed away. Isaac himself barely survives to tell the tale but his house too is destroyed, and although Isaac tries to hold onto his wife Cora, she is lost to the devastation.

It is a wonderful book; a true story, and it is beautifully told by Larson.

I rode out to see the memorial statue located on the seawall at 47th street. The 'Great Storm' as it now called is still the greatest natural disaster to occur in the United States. The ten-foot-tall bronze sculpture portrays a family - a father, mother, and child - clinging together. One of the man's arms is reaching for the sky, and the other is around his wife. She is cradling their baby in her arms.

Of course, Galveston has been rebuilt since then. On higher ground I am assured and with a substantial sea wall that provides defence against the hurricanes that are a seasonal threat in the area. Galveston has also been beautified by the addition of a 'While You Wait One Hour Lube' outlet, a Wendy's burger joint and an always busy Chick-Fil-A.

All of the accommodation on Galveston Island was aimed at tourists. They, unlike me, were all there to enjoy the beach and spend big. It was too rich for this poor and famously miserly, old biker. So, I rode out to the lookout at San Jacinto point on the very eastern promontory of the island to make the most of my last moments in Galveston. I watched the seemingly endless procession of oil tankers in the channel. Some taking Texas oil away from the refineries and some bringing goods and cargo into the port.

I rode along the dock road to see if any cruise ships were already docked there, but all of the massive berths were empty, so I rode back across the bridge, back to the mainland, and almost immediately saved myself close to one-hundred books by checking into a motel on the mainland for less than forty dollars. It was damp, cramped and smelled of death. Perfection.

Piggly Wiggly

There was no breakfast in the lobby of the Motel. To be fair, for the price, I had been grateful that there had actually been a bed and a toilet that at least pretended to flush, even if it had no effect whatsoever on the contents I had deposited there.

So, without both morning sustenance and the potential of a future lunch I checked the bike over, loaded my kit and set off into the already rising heat of the morning.

I rode along a road punctuated by vast expanses of water. This was a green and humid land replete with languid rivers and large lakes. Where the tributaries ran slow, they had created the famous bayous, large flat areas of semi-stagnant and brackish water that teemed with wildlife. Tall cypress trees were clothed in Spanish moss.

The Spanish moss hung in heavy clumps, from the crowns of the trees down towards the water that sparkled with the delicate touch of a thousand dragonflies.

Spanish moss isn't in fact Spanish. It is not even a moss. It was first named by the native American Indians who called it '*itla-okla*,' which meant tree hair, for so it surely resembles. The French, when they arrived in the region thought that it looked like the long grey beards of the conquistadors and named it Spanish beard, and over time the name changed to the Spanish moss that we know it as today.

The morning was already stiflingly hot and desperately humid. I tried to ride with the visor up, but the bugs were thick in the southern heat, drawn by the cool and the reek of the bayous that I passed on either side. I got off the interstate at the town of Winnie and headed back towards the coast to see if the breeze from the gulf might bring me some relief.

State Road 73 took me eastward to the town of Port Arthur where I crossed the Sabine Lake on the Sabine Lake Causeway Bridge. On the other side I found myself finally free of Texas. I gave a little cheer and stood up on the foot pegs, raising a hand of salute in relief.

I was back in Louisiana – the land of Union, Justice and Confidence according to the state motto.

You need a certain amount of confidence to live near the coast in Louisiana. It is estimated that close to fifty percent of the entire state is below sea level. Given the threat of global warming and rising sea levels and a levee system that was never designed to operate cohesively, that percentage seems certain to increase.

The levees were built in this region from different types of construction, of differing sizes and with different landowners over a two-hundred-year period. Unlike the dykes built by the Dutch engineers, they define impermanence.

The gulf coast was pretty enough and thankfully a good few degrees cooler, but oil refineries and storage facilities rose to scar the otherwise pristine skyline.

All day long I rattled over old bridges and skirted vast wildlife reserves and inland waterways. Small cabins and ranch houses were dotted along the road, their roofs bleached by the unrelenting beat of the sun, siding peeling in the corrosive salt tang of the air. An old rusting Ford or a Chevy parked in each drive.

Close to the town of Pecan Island the road swept me north, away from the coast. I had not seen so many small lakes and waterways since I had ridden through Finland many years before. For most of the day I saw not a soul as I sweated away in my heavy jacket and helmet.

I stopped at a Piggly Wiggly on the outskirts of La Fayette. Piggly Wiggly was the first true self-service grocery store in the world. It introduced shoppers to the now common practice of browsing and picking their own groceries. Prior to the invention of Piggly Wiggly shoppers queued at a counter and waited for the salesperson to first select and then bag the groceries they requested.

Piggly Wiggly are dotted all across the south and they are always worth a visit. Nobody really knows where the name came from but there is a clever range of merchandise that supports the brand.

I stepped inside to enjoy the icy blast of the air conditioning and to buy two chilled bottles of water.

I stood panting and red-faced in the sudden darkened shade of the store, directly beneath a rattling air-conditioning vent while I gulped the water down a dry throat, my Adam's apple bobbing like a kid on Guy Fawkes's night. I placed the two empty bottles on the counter and croaked out a raspy, "just these please."

The rather large black lady seated there, looked at me with a look usually reserved for lost children, simpletons, and the insane. She scanned me up and down. Slowly. From my dusty boots to my damp and bedraggled scarlet coloured face. A vein was throbbing in my temple, and she stared at that for several seconds, surely wondering when it would pop and collapse me to the floor at her feet.

She shook her head in pity and said in one long, slow drawl, "is you ok honey? Coz you look like sumbody should be look'n after you."

How rude. I gave her a tight British smile and muttered back, "I'm fine thank you," and staggered reluctantly back into the blast of the furnace.

The day was interminable. The ride seemingly never ending. I was tired and far too hot. My skin itched under the jacket. Sweat flowed in a hot and steady stream down my back and arms. My eyes stung from the relentless drip of salt sweat from my brow. The heat came from all directions. From the sun that hung like a heat lamp directly above me, but also from the Suzuki, and the road at my wheels, that reflected the heat back like the devil himself was rising from his underworld, bringing his hell and brimstone to seize the soul of a mad dog and this errant Englishman.

I had hoped to reach New Orleans. But then I remembered that I absolutely detested the place and wondered, not for the first time, what gene of intelligence I was deficient in that possessed me to make these crazy decisions. It wasn't as if I didn't already know about the place. Like

Las Vegas, it is on my list of places I never need to see again as long as I live.

In 2023, New Orleans was labelled the 'Murder Capital' of the entire country by an NBC News report. Overall, New Orleans ranks thirteenth in violent crimes, fourth in murder, and second in rape. It really has it all for the lonely tourist.

Bourbon Street is a hell hole of debauchery and filth. The French quarter is somewhat better, but all accommodation at this time of year would be expensive, and where on earth in such a city could I safely leave the bike and all of my belongings, never mind my good self.

I pulled over by the side of the road, raising a curtain of dust as I dragged my left foot to a stop. I looked at the map while I slicked the sweat from a throbbing temple with a bare hand. The road to New Orleans actually took me south, out of my way, so even if New Orleans had not been the stabby death trap that I knew it to be, that alone made up my mind for me.

About fifty miles ahead lay a strip of small towns that were spread out along the gulf coast to the east of New Orleans. There was sure to be accommodation there. It would have to do. I was beaten by the heat and too tired to think of any better option. So, I carefully refolded my map. I pulled my clammy helmet back on to a sweaty head with some difficulty and pulled away to eat up the last of the miles.

That last hour may have been one of the worst experiences on a motorcycle I have ever had. The baking heat of the day became suffocation as the humidity spiked. It was like riding through hot swampy bathwater. My headache intensified until I was screwing up my eyes behind a visor drenched in condensation against the throb. The sun was still high in a clear cerulean sky, but I don't think I could have been wetter if I had ridden through a monsoon in just my lucky batman underpants.

The minutes ticked by and now I was focussed on the mile markers that counted down my approach to the end of the day. Knowing precisely how far I still needed to ride just made any progress seem slower, a literal watched pot.

I crossed the Mississippi river and used the ring road to avoid the clamour of Baton Rouge and then headed east, back towards the coast.

I rode around the northern edge of the massive Lake Pontchartain and almost immediately crossed back into Mississippi. Thirty-five minutes later, and with a huge sigh of relief I finally caught the familiar twinkle of the Gulf of Mexico, a thin line of blue on the horizon.

I took the next exit and immediately found a little oasis of cheap and nasty looking hotels close to Gulfport, that clamoured around a rather grand looking Holiday Inn like seagulls around a fancy beachside landfill.

For once I completely ignored the opportunity to save a few bucks. I desperately needed aggressive air conditioning, the kind that puckers skin, a shower that sprays more than three drops of lukewarm, rusty water an hour, and a mattress that didn't seethe with unwanted life beneath me, and with at least some of its springs still in place.

I also need a hotel with extensive room service and a full bar. I pulled the hot Suzuki into the Holiday Inn car park muttering, "fuck the expense. I'm worth it."

When I finally manged to prise my eyelids apart in the morning, my bedroom in the Holiday Inn looked like one Keith Moon and Roger Daltrey had partied in. My filthy, sweaty kit lay in piles around the room. You could trace my steps as I entered the room the evening prior, as I had quickly and desperately discarded hot and dusty clothing. By the door still lay my boots and gloves, followed by pants and a riding jacket and then, closer to the bathroom, a soiled, still damp t-shirt. And then, just inside the door of the bathroom a pair of socks and my lucky underpants, the last sweat-stained items to be discarded before I fell under the glorious, icy cold spell of the power shower for close on an hour.

There were empty beer bottles rolling around on the dresser and a room service tray whose few remaining tattered contents suggested a bear attack might have recently taken place. All that remained were the signs of a feast enjoyed. Empty ketchup sachets, soiled napkins, and the remains of two or three fries that had once accompanied the double stacker cheeseburger, lay scattered across the tray.

The room stank of fries, vinegar and grease. I tentatively sniffed an armpit. I stank of fries, vinegar and grease. I was also cold, shivering even. I had slept naked on the bed, with the covers around only my toes, basking in the hum of the glorious air-conditioning.

I got up and put the coffee maker on while I took another shower, this one hot, to wake and cleanse me and to take some of the unwanted chill away.

Under the shower I emptied all of the miniature bottles of shower, gel, shampoo and conditioner onto my self and scrubbed the tiny bar of soap on dirty pores until it was small enough to clog the drain. I then towelled myself dry with every one of the white fluffy towels and then walked back into the bedroom in the free slippers and wrapped in my robe like a sultan prince.

I slowly worked my way through all of the crappy breakfast teas that surely nobody really enjoys, and poured all of the sugars and creamers into the several cups of coffee until it was all gone. I had used and abused everything I had paid for.

I found my least dirty pair of pants and a shirt, made sure that my helmet was as empty as it was possible to be and then walked down the stairs with it in my hands like a bowl to get breakfast and my free lunch.

It was ready to start the last few miles towards Atlanta and home.

Outside the sun was hiding behind some thick clouds and I breathed a sigh of relief. The first part of my ride would take me first eastward along the coast, but the majority of my ride would be almost due north. But I was still in the deep south, and while I expected the humidity to ease slightly on my long ride home, if the sun did make an appearance, the heat index would be similar to the previous day.

With the end of the long ride finally in sight, I didn't spare the horses. Today was not a day for sightseeing and distractions. I picked up the interstate and hunkered down behind the tall screen and accelerated thorough the gears along the coast.

Twenty minutes later I crossed into Alabama close to Mobile and immediately my path swept me northwards. Around lunchtime I stopped at a rest place and ate my stolen sandwich and some fruit and gulped a bottle of water. As I left Montgomery, I picked up I-85.

I let out a long sigh. This was my road, the road that would take me all the way up and through Atlanta, into the suburbs north of the city. It took all of my self-control to keep close to the posted speed limits and not race home to the life of ease and comfort that awaited me.

Close to Westpoint I crossed into Georgia with a little yelp of delight and then ninety minutes later the sky filled with passenger jets. Hartsfield Jackson International Airport. Atlanta airport, the busiest in the world. It took me an hour more to cover the last twenty-five miles. Traffic is always a nightmare in Atlanta, twenty-four hours a day, three-hundred, and sixty-five days a year, and remember no lane splitting. But sixty minutes later I rode the little Suzuki V-Strom up the hill that led to my house and killed the engine. I sat for a long second listening to the pinking of the cooling engine and then kicked down the stand and walked inside to see if my wife and dogs still recognised me.

Pensacola

Back at home, I made loafing around and generally getting in the way look like an Olympic sport. In the evenings I dozed, watching Larry the Cable Guy repeats on the TV, with Archie, my dog sprawled on my knee, and then slept luxuriously late into the morning in my super king bed, spread out, arms and legs akimbo like some exhausted giant star fish.

I followed my long-suffering wife around the house like a lovesick puppy, asking her mundane questions about the likelihood of her making me another sandwich and what the contents of said sandwich might include, while she prodded my filthy clothes into the washing machine with a stick barely long enough to keep the wildness and stench at bay.

I did some sausage jobs around the house. Sausage jobs include trash removal, the mowing of lawns, pest control, and the sprinkling of random but always significantly large amounts of chemicals into the swimming pool to keep it from returning to its natural state of being a frog filled swamp.

Life at home was comfortable and easy. I got lunch with my wife and chilled out, enjoying the ease and cool of the house. Work seemed to have completely given up on me. They had moved on without me. After twenty years for the same firm, in two different countries and in a somewhat senior position, it was suddenly as if I had never worked there. As my boss had suggested, the changes the company was going through effectively made me invisible. Nobody knew where I was or what I was, or was not, doing. It was bliss. Over the years the company had extracted its pound of flesh from me. It was time to get some payback.

The days passed slowly but Ben's graduation loomed ever closer and unfortunately, it was soon time to get back on the bike and ride south again.

I would ride first to Pensacola on the Florida panhandle to see Ben graduate, and then head east to strike across country to reach the Atlantic coast and the city of Jacksonville. If all went well, I would hopefully be in time to see Ben board the aircraft carrier that would speed him eastward towards his first proper command in Japan.

Our time in America too was coming to a suddenly abrupt end. We had finally decided to leave. The house was already listed for sale. We were busy scouring Idealista, a Spanish version of Right Move, trying to find a villa in Spain that would provide us with a suitable short-term lease to allow us to begin the move to Spain. The company I still, kind of worked for, may have overlooked me for the moment but it couldn't last for ever. It would soon be time to formally retire, and when I did it would mean the end of our healthcare benefits.

I changed the oil and the oil filter on the V-Strom. Cleaned, adjusted, and oiled the chain and added a few PSI to the tires. The bike had stood up impressively to so many miles in such a short space of time. The bike suited me well and where on initial inspection I had thought the seat height too high for my stretching toe caps, I now thought that the bike was perfect. We were well suited, this somewhat old chap who stood a touch on the short side and this lofty and comfortable adventurer.

The very next morning I packed my top box and hard panniers with newly fragranced and freshened underwear and got ready to depart. Paula would be driving the car south and for at least the first few miles I would be following.

We cut through the heart of the city I had grown used to calling home. I rode past the King and Queen buildings, through the interminable roadworks, close to the busy intersection with the ring road, I-285, that encircles Atlanta. I kept the Georgia Tech campus on my right to join the six slow lanes of traffic on I-85 south.

I passed the Varsity, the somewhat famous hotdog eatery that looks down onto the interstate, rode slowly past Emory Hospital and then Grady, reminding myself once again that Emory is the place to go if you urgently need an organ to be transplanted and Grady is the place to head to if you were ever careless enough in Atlanta to receive a gunshot wound, and were capable, and still suitably replete with blood to keep on walking and talking.

The sky slowly filled with passenger jets as it always does, and then we broke free of the city, heading past the craziness of Hartsfield-Jackson airport, the place I had spent so many hours of my life, either waiting for a plane to fly me out to some bullshit meeting, or back, kerbside, sweating in the evening heat, silently waiting for an Uber to take me home again.

Free of the city at last, the road narrowed to two lanes, but I still managed to pick up the pace. I passed Paula with a wave outside of the town of Locust Grove and gunned the Suzuki to generate some fast-moving, cooling air across the radiator and up the arms of my jacket.

The sun blazed in a perfectly cloudless sky. The miles rolled by. Southern Georgia is a land defined by its history. It is a mostly flat arable country filled with the cottonfields of its heritage.

I first made this journey with the family when we were all younger, south through the state of Georgia to vacation in Florida, almost fifteen years ago. It was soon after we first arrived in the United States, and I had been filled with excitement.

I had pictured soft Georgia hills festooned with beaming white marble antebellum homes at the end of long drives. I expected to see a portly gentlemen seated on a swing on one of the elegant front porches, dressed in a white suit and smoking a black cheroot while sipping on a mint julep.

Unfortunately, modern southern Georgia is an amalgam of endless roadside outlets selling Vidalia onions and pecans. The remote farmsteads still fly the occasional but unnerving confederate flag and the massive billboards that line the roadside alternatively advertise Jesus (yes, he is still coming apparently), appallingly worded anti-abortion rhetoric 'Abortion hurts mothers and murders there babies,' or how many miles you needed to wait until you could finally buy that dildo, the one with the realistic throbbing veins, the one you had been thinking about upgrading to at the next adult sex store.

Jesus, Abortion, Dildos, Jesus, Abortion, Dildos, Jesus, Abortion, Dildos. It all gets very confusing very quickly in the deep south.

As I rode, the heat just got more intense, and the humidity flew off the charts to create a continuous river of sweat down all of the cracks that the last few months riding the bike had blessed me with.

I had to pull off the interstate to get some gas for the bike just as I crossed the line into Dooley County. As I believe I have previously mentioned, the USA has this odd and annoying habit of not having filling stations inside the rest places that are positioned every thirty or forty miles or so along the Interstate itself. Instead, motorists have to turn off the interstate and then drive, often to the nearest town, to fill up with gas.

I did that now, following some signs for a Conoco gas station. The road took me over a creek and down a very rural back country road. In the shanty homes that lined the road, each yard had at least one broken down pickup truck in the front yard. Every mailbox was in the form of either a manatee or a large fish stood on its hind fins. MAGA and the occasional confederate flag fluttered in the fetid air, strewn from almost every broken-down porch.

There were no signs of working farms, no factories, no shops, no commerce. What folks here did for gainful employment, and what paid the taxes in Dooley County was a mystery to me.

I rode through a tunnel of Spanish Moss that hung like untidy grey beards from the trees above me. Cicadas chittered in the trees. The humidity was devastating. I was soaked in my own sweat, head banging with the onset of another dehydration.

I finally found the gas station and pulled in to park the bike close to the nearest pump. I had to wait for the attendant to come pump the gas for me. He was just finishing filling a rusty Ford pickup that had once been painted red. A streak of rusty brown mysteriously marred the side of the truck, from the passenger side window all the way back to the tailgate. On the tailgate of the pickup was a very old and faded Harley Davidson sticker.

Inside the pickup, the two sleeveless denim shirted occupants stared at me through their cracked and grimy windscreen, while I removed my helmet and dragged the dirty sleeve of my riding jacket across my sweat-beaded forehead. I nodded a friendly hello at them, but they just sent a dead fish-eye stare back in my direction.

Finally, one of the country boys slowly and manually wound down his side window. The windowpane gave a loud squeal of protest. My new country friend slowly rested a pale slab of forearm on the door frame and leant his head out.

"That there one of em Soo-zoo-keeees?" He said, almost taking a breath between each word that slipped like molasses from his lips.

I could only assume he was talking to me, but he had been blessed with one very lazy eye, and could have been talking either to me, his partner seated next to him or even his God in his heaven.

"It sure is," I grinned back cheerfully enough.

His jaw and tongue worked around the ball of tobacco he had been chewing for several long seconds, while he slowly processed this information. Even the cicadas had fallen silent, as if they too waited with bated breath for the next piece of wisdom he would utter.

Finally, he emitted a slow noise, "hmmm...hmmm." He gave one last long rumination and made a little 'O' shape out the side of his mouth. He then hawked a ball of foul black glistening tobacco onto the ground at the side of his truck. It wasn't the best spit and some of the goo trickled down the side of the truck's door, immediately explaining the strange rust-coloured markings on the vehicle.

He continued to stare at three things at once as he gradually wound his side window back up.

While I stood transfixed by this bizarre exchange, some kind of fly bit me on the back of the neck. I slapped the area with my gloved hand and realized that the gas station was inundated with buzzing, swarming, black flies. I had no idea what they were, but they were voracious and angry. They swarmed all around me. A loud humming sound drew my attention to a bucket by one of the pumps. These buckets are usually filled with clean sudsy water with a nearby handheld squeegee on hand, to allow motorists to wipe clean a dusty windscreen, but this bucket was a roiling mass of furious flies.

There were so many flies, the bucket must have been filled with shit or possibly something even worse. The decapitated head of the last motorcyclist with the temerity to ride a Japanese motorcycle through Dooley County perhaps? My nose wrinkled and I pulled my helmet back on. I strolled in a very casual, I am unconcerned by the events taking place manner, as I could back to the bike.

I am not normally out of place somewhere, especially in America. By this time, it had been my home for a good percentage of my adult life, and, for the bigger part, I love the country. I had always been welcomed everywhere I had visited with a warm smile, an interested enquiry of where, and why I was riding somewhere, and usually, an offer of assistance if I needed it.

But something was very off here, in this strange little backwater.

The attendant was done with the pickup, and he finally walked across to me. Despite being filled, the pickup still hadn't moved away and the boys in front were still sending me daggers.

I nodded to the attendant to fill her up. I stared back at the occupants of the pickup to make sure they knew I was quite the tough character myself. I did once take two or three junior Karate lessons in a YMCA, so I was pretty handy with the old fisticuffs if needs arose, but even so my heart began to beat a little too fast.

As soon as the pump cut off, I handed the attendant a twenty-dollar bill. I closed the filler cap, swung a leg over the bike and accelerated hard back down the road, back in the direction of the Interstate.

All the way back to the Interstate, I kept one eye in the mirror, looking for a plume of dust on the horizon, to make sure nobody had followed me. I was quite spooked, which is very unusual.

It was probably nothing, just some bad luck in picking such a shithole place to choose to fill up in, and, at the same time to stumble upon a couple of such rural wankers wanting to give the non-Harley riding biker a hard time.

It occurred to me, not for the for first time, that despite my undeniable privilege as a heterosexual middle aged white guy, I had still been made to feel acutely uncomfortable in a country I was a happy citizen of. One I was normally proud to call my own.

I had to wonder what kind of reception a person of colour, a gay person, or any minority really would have received from these wonky eyed shitkickers.

I was still thinking about the strange encounter when I re-joined the Interstate. I needed to clear the air, to put some distance between me and the bad feeling. I rolled the throttle back a little too aggressively to merge into heavy traffic and to quickly pass a big semi-tractor trailer. As soon as I got into the fast lane I saw, too late, the dark black cruiser parked on the hard shoulder. I glanced in my mirrors, and my heart sank as I saw him accelerate hard away from the shoulder and light up his blues and twos.

I let him have an easy catch. I pulled into the inside lane, still slightly optimistically hoping he might be responding to an emergency call further up the road. But as soon as he pulled in behind me, I indicated right and pulled over onto the hard shoulder and turned off the bike. I put my hands in clear view on the tank in front of me, which is the wise thing to do when stopped by the police in America. I am not advocating compliancy, but it is a habit that will, generally, keep you from being shot dead by the roadside by a young and jumpy cop.

It turned out he was a decent sort, albeit dressed like Officer Rosco P. Coltrane as he was. He wore the overly large headgear of the State Trooper. It looked ridiculous to me, a ten-gallon hat on a two-pint head, but he seemed to wear it with pride and smiled with satisfaction at having shot one more fish in the barrel as he grinned a row of white teeth, eyes hidden behind his reflective aviator shades.

He began to give me the usual sarcastic lecture that all traffic policeman across the globe must get trained to deliver.

But, before he got too far into his practiced lecture, I admitted my mistake and also somewhat casually let slip into the conversation that I was in a rush because I was desperately proud and wanted to see my eldest son depart on his first posting in the U.S. Navy.

Americans to their credit are nothing if not entirely patriotic. I guess it can work both ways. With the googly eyed interbred dumb fucks in the pickup truck, it had worked against me. A complete change of attitude with Roscoe P. Coltrane here. The cop let me off the super speeder ticker which I had surely earned, and which would likely necessitate a visit all the way back to Dooley fucking County to have it enforced. I got away with a small fine, a mild ticking off and a, "thank your son for his service for me OK sir," as he waved me on my way.

As I rode more slowly away, I realised I had stumbled upon the only major source of income for the residents of Dooley County. Outside of revenue for fining travellers for traffic violations there was absolutely no money at all coming in from anywhere else.

It was with a deep sigh of relief that I crossed the county line and left Dooley far behind me.

At West Point I crossed the southern loop of the Chattahoochee River and back once more into Sweet Home Alabama, and that bloody guitar refrain began twanging away in the back of my head once again.

I pulled off the interstate at the town of Tuskegee and rode across to park the pinging, pinking Suzuki outside city hall. The name '*Tuskegee*' comes from the native American Muskogee word '*Taskeke,*' which very aptly means '*warriors*.'

The Tuskegee Airmen were the first African American military aviators in the United States Armed Forces. They flew both fighters and bombers to great aplomb and glory in World War Two.

I thought that close to city hall I would be certain to find a commemorative statue to the airmen but there was nothing there. The only statue on show was one dedicated to the Confederate soldiers who fought for the south in the Civil War. The only monument to the Tuskegee airmen is, strangely, located in South Carolina, not the town where they originated.

It is fair to say that despite the airmen being hailed as war heroes they were still subjected to the racial segregation of the archaic Jim Crow laws that lingered.

While living in America, I had heard the phrase Jim Crow for years, but genuinely had no idea who or what Jim Crow was, so, to simultaneously rectify my ignorance and intensify guilt I didn't know I should have had, I looked it all up.

The Jim Crow laws were a bunch of state and local laws introduced in the Southern United States in the late 19th and early 20th centuries that enforced racial segregation. It turns out that 'Jim Crow' was a pejorative term for an African American.

The name Jim Crow was derived from a theatre character developed by entertainer Thomas D. Rice. It was popularized through his black and white minstrel shows that my much older readers may remember that we used to innocently enjoy when I was a boy. But the character is a degrading and hurtful stereotypical depiction of African Americans and of their culture.

In practice, Jim Crow laws mandated racial segregation throughout all of the public facilities in the states of the former confederacy, and in some others, beginning in the 1870s and continuing...well...from what I had experienced first-hand, and what I had been told by my black friends...to the current day.

OK. Perhaps not the *physical* segregation. Those laws *have* thankfully been repealed. But the minds and attitudes of a persistently hard-core set of the white folks in the deep south, those principles, those dearly held beliefs, those biases, those discriminatory ideals. Those can still leave a lot to be desired.

And remember none of this is a vague and distant memory. Something yet to be told by a dusty old professor in history 101. This is far from being ancient history separated from those of us living today by the sins of our great, great grandfathers. The last law of segregation was repealed in 1964 when sweeping Federal laws prohibited such discrimination.

Discrimination is still alive and well in the deep south, and, as much as I love the place, outside of the urban centres of places like Atlanta, where the high-tech companies have drawn an ethnically diverse workforce to live and work in their modern cities, you only need to travel thirty-miles in any direction, and you can achieve the miracle of time travel and quickly find yourself all the way back in the 1920s.

Phew. That was a lot of serious stuff. I apologize. As if to make amends I now found myself hopelessly lost in a sandy delta of criss-crossing back roads. I had shunned the highway back at the town of Evergreen and was still fairly certain I was heading towards Pensacola and the Gulf Coast, but all of the road signs had disappeared, and I had entirely lost my sense of direction.

I passed a sign telling me that I was no longer in Alabama and had crossed into Florida, which was a good thing. But I must have taken a wrong turn somewhere as I now found myself on a very rural road indeed. There were just a few struggling farms dotted across the broad but empty fields. A fine layer of sand blew cross the road which made me think that I might be getting closer to the coast, but then I rounded a bend and the road just ended at some railroad tracks. On the other side of the railway lines was a road that quickly petered out into a dusty path ingrained with deep tyre tracks.

I turned the bike around with some tippy-toe athleticism and started to head back in the direction I had arrived to find a local fellow looking at me from over his hedge.

I rode the bike across and lifted my visor.

"Good afternoon," I shouted, "can you point me in the direction of Pensacola."

Nothing. Not a single blink or muscle twitch to show that he had heard me or was even aware of my presence.

I shouted louder, "excuse me. Sir?"

More nothing.

I can only assume he was Florida's version of what we rather disparagingly called a bumpkin when I lived in Somerset. Someone who flagged that a nearby village might be missing its idiot.

"Thanks anyway," I shouted sarcastically with a cheery wave and set off back down the road.

I then made some random turns which is my habit when I am lost. It's not a great tactic as I now found that I no longer even had a clue in which direction south lay. The sun was of no help as it hung directly above me, and moss grew thickly on every side of every tree.

It was of no surprise that ten minutes later I found myself back in Alabama close to the town of Canoe. I pulled over to check the map and figured out where I had gone wrong.

I took State Road 31 east for a few miles and crossed back into Florida at Flomaton.

Forty minutes later, sweaty, overheated, tired and more than a touch crotchety, I crossed the bridge over Pensacola Bay and took the State Road 98 coast road east to arrive in the pretty town of Pensacola. Pensacola sits on what is known as the panhandle of America. The panhandle is a long strip of very expensive coastal real estate that encompasses much of the northern shore of the Gulf of Mexico.

The sight that greeted me reminded me that I had arrived in the part of America even the rednecks in these parts call, '*The Redneck Riviera.*' I had seen less pickups in the car park of a monster truck rally. But unlike the tobacco spit stained Ford from Dooley County, these trucks belonged to a different class of bib-overall wearing folks.

The good people here all looked and talked like rednecks, but these here rednecks were filthy fucking rich y'all. Brand new Ford F-150s, Dodge RAMs, and Chevy Silverados lined the boulevards and filled the municipal car parks. Besides every other truck was a boat trailer.

Unlike the poor and inbred shitkickers from Dooley County, these folks dressed like rednecks because they admired the look. But these wifebeater T-shirts and shorts weren't bought from the dollar store out of necessity, these were carefully tailored by Fred Perry and Von Maur and purchased from Macys at cost. These folks were like Larry the Cable Guy, adopting a façade that hid the fact that they all lived in wealthy neighbourhoods in the metropolitan areas of Louisiana and Mississippi and were vacationing from their well-paid jobs as dentists and lawyers.

There were very few missing teeth, all eyes pointed, for the best part in the same direction, and almost all of the tattoos were spelt correctly. This was the elite. The royalty. The Platinum Club of the south.

Other than that though, it felt uncannily like being back at a millionaire's version of Talladega and I gave a little involuntary shudder of despair as I recalled that experience.

I rode east away from town and, having stuck to the interstate I found that Paula had easily beaten me to the small, but very sweet little coastal AirBnB we had rented for a couple of nights.

Ten minutes after I arrived, and after I had thankfully parked the bike in the little covered garage below the apartment, what usually happens at four in the afternoon in Florida inevitably happened. The sun disappeared, the clouds clustered, thunder rumbled, and the heavens absolutely opened to dump their considerably soggy contents in a tumultuous ten-minute drenching deluge.

I stood on the balcony with a can of Stella in hand, watching the almost impenetrable curtain of rain sweep across the beach in front of me. Lightning forked and crackled; and thunder boomed with sufficient ferocity to rattle the windows.

And then the ferocious storm system, stoked into virile life by the warmth of the Gulf, simply moved on down the coast to drench Tampa and Fort Myers, leaving Pensacola baked once more in a ferocious sunshine that turned the puddles into steaming cauldrons of evaporation.

In the morning, we drove around the headland to the Naval Air Station at Pensacola. The waters of the gulf were a ridiculous shade of aquamarine. The sands shone burnished gold. The sea broke itself into crystal clear white shards on the perfect shoreline.

It was so clear, and clean, and pretty it shocked my English brain. Where were the one-legged seagulls with used condoms clasped in their beaks, where were the muddy estuaries, the broken sandcastle buckets, and abandoned shopping trolleys. Where oh where, was the fog and freezing horizontal rain?

At the security gates of the Naval Air Station, we had our very first experience of security on an operational military base. Ben had not left our names at the security gate as he should have done for visiting relatives, so we were forced to drive out of the long line of cars and to park up and have our driver's licenses taken for inspection.

Finally, the Military Policeman gave us a placard with directions on, which would also serve as a parking permit and waved us through. The base was huge. Long, wide roads led between buildings, both residential and industrial. We even had to cross a full-size golf course. As we drove through the base, still trying to navigate, the loudest roar I have ever heard made us jump out of our seats and duck involuntarily.

To our left, almost within touching distance, streaking low across the arc of the bay, were six F18 Super Hornets. It was the Blue Falcons display team, America's version of the British Red Arrows, who were based at Pensacola, practicing the low pass manoeuvre they would demonstrate at their next air show.

We finally found the correct building and parked up. Ben had seen us and walked out with a friend of his.

That evening we found a little seaside shack and together we ate a mountain of peel and eat shrimp and drank several icy cold beers as the sun set over the Gulf Coast, while we watched a pod of dolphins breaking the water with arched slippery grey backs. As the shiny dorsal fins dipped back below the perfectly still surface, they made large concentric circles in the water that continued to move outward and grow, until they exhausted the small energy the dolphins had relinquished and slowly disappeared.

Heaven.

Another Farewell

When I first moved to the USA, I loved it when I had to work in Florida. I loved arriving by aeroplane to be suddenly immersed in the palm trees, the open waterways, the endless blue skies, the golden sands, and the crystal blue seas, so warm it feels like taking a pee in an already hot bath. I honestly thought I would actually retire there one day. And then I realized a few things about the state that made me reconsider.

For those who haven't been unlucky enough to spend some time in real Florida, and here we do not count Disneyland, the true constants that make the Sunshine State are the startling number of weird, walnut, leather-skinned, white-haired pony-tailed dudes and dudesses who haunt every intersection, cigarette held in nicotine-stained hands, muttering to themselves.

Florida is also defined by the plethora of Chinese manufactured MAGA stickers on the trucks and fluttering red, white, and blue pennants on the immaculate lawns. The state of Florida is deeply republican. It is home to Trump and Mar-A-Lago, and the famously pro-Christian, anti-abortion state senator Ron DeSantis

Florida is also filled to the brim with 'snowbirds.' Snowbirds represent the most wrinkled and antiquated and usually quietly wealthy people in America. They migrate like geese to Florida, all sheltering from the cold winds and snows of the north. They hunch over the gigantic steering wheels of their enormous Plymouths and Cadillacs, glaucoma muddied eyes peering two inches from their windscreens, entirely oblivious and possibly blind to the proximity of any other road users. I don't believe any of them have even seen a motorcycle in the past twenty years.

Florida is also home to Alligators. They live in the swamps and the waterways of course. But they also live right there amongst the subdivisions, in the ponds and creeks, patiently waiting for an unwary child or a juicy Chihuahua to wander by. There are, on average, eight alligator attacks each year in Florida. There are forty-six types of snakes that are native to Florida and two-hundred and fifty species of spiders. And of course, there are the Palmetto bugs and the Lovebugs.

The name Palmetto bug, after all, has a pretty ring to it. Like a Ladybird or a butterfly perhaps. Think again. I can only assume that the name Palmetto bug was coined by the Floridian tourist board to conceal the fact that they are in fact, cockroaches.

But, in the same way that Peter Parker is neither an ordinary man, nor an ordinary spider, Palmetto bugs are not ordinary cockroaches. Palmetto bugs are a particularly scary version of cockroach that has evolved the ability to take to the wing.

Instead of only being able to scuttle around in a freakish and terrifying manner like land-based cockroaches, Palmetto bugs can terrorize from the skies. They drop, without warning, onto heads to writhe and become tangled into hair, or to land on plates of shrimp and make diners squeal and leap to feet. But be careful if you disturb a Palmetto bug, because, when startled, a Palmetto bug will spray a foul-smelling liquid up to four feet in your direction, totally ruining the aroma and allure of your expensive Brut cologne.

Palmetto bugs might be so named by the Florida tourist board and, perhaps, one or two confused entomologists, but true Floridians call them skunk, or stink roaches.

The only thing worse than a Palmetto bug is a Lovebug. I assumed that a Lovebug was some kind of adorable Volkswagen with a personality and a mind of its own. But I was, once again, proved wrong. I found out what a Lovebug was to my horror, the very next day, on the ride across Florida on I-10 travelling west to east, from Pensacola to Jacksonville.

I was busy bumbling along on the V-Strom. The sun, as it always is in Florida was high in the perfectly blue sky. The sun doesn't rise or set in Florida. It just appears each morning, at the very highest point of the sky, blazing down mercilessly to paint the polished bald domes of pale Englishmen a bright and tender vermillion red.

Up ahead, on the two-lane freeway was the usual mix of eighteen wheelers, pickup trucks and holidaymakers, cars jam packed with suitcases, pillows and Maui Jim surf shop coloured swimming shorts and Hawaiian shirts. The trees of the Osceola National Forest clustered up close to the highway, the watery flash of the mangrove swamps visible now and again through the gaps.

My attention was drawn to what appeared to be a line of smoke drifting across the road, perhaps half a mile in the distance. It hung in the humid air about a meter in height above the road, a thin but dense black smudge. I looked to both sides of the road to see if a car was on fire on the roadside, or if a Floridian farmer in this desolate landscape had finally despaired and committed self-immolation in one of his perennially flooded and crocodile infested fields. But there was no sign of a conflagration.

The dark line grew thicker and darker as I got closer, but none of the traffic ahead seemed to notice. No brake lights or signs of slowing, so I just screwed up my eyes in confusion and kept rolling back the throttle.

As I got closer a bug hit dead centre of my visor with quite the thwack that rocked my head back a few millimetres. It instantly turned itself from black, winged and buzzing, to red, blobbed and dead.

"Christ on a bike," I muttered.

And then another hit. And then another. And then I hit the edge of the smudge.

Suddenly I was riding at speed through a dense cloud of Lovebugs. They spattered like heavy horizontal rain and rattled like hail on a cheap caravan roof across the fairing, the screen, my visor, and whatever parts of me lay outside the limited protection they afforded.

But unlike rain or hail, the bugs exploded on impact and each one turned into a tiny blood-filled paintball bullet. My head was rocked by each impact and the visor soon became so congealed with exploded corpses that I had to strain to see. It was if somebody had instantly pulled a bank robbers sixty-denier stocking over the top of my helmet. I wiped a gloved hand across the visor in an attempt to clear the carnage but succeeded only in smearing the individual impacts into one scarlet and tiny insectile leg and wing filled porridge.

I had no choice but to lift the visor and fumble in the sudden darkness to finally hit the switch for the hazard lights to slow and begin to pull over to the roadside. The bugs continued to hit me but now they struck my unprotected face. They were instantly in my blinking eyes, puckered nostrils and teeth, pulled back from lips, that were magically transformed into something resembling a fuzzy black gum shield.

At the side of the road, I got off the bike and danced around like a crazy person, brushing the dead bugs off my jacket and shaking tiny corpses out of folds and crevices. I had a bottle of water in the top box, and with an old hanky, I managed to rinse my eyes, scrub my face, the visor, and a very small part of the bike's screen at least somewhat clean.

As I had worked, the cloud of bugs magically disappeared as if they had never been there.

I learned later that these Lovebugs are fast becoming the scourge of Florida. They are an invasive species and are distasteful to birds, so they have no natural predators and, of course, being Lovebugs they breed prodigiously.

For all motorists, they are a problem as they are attracted by the rising heat of the highways and tend to congregate, En-masse in those very locations that we tend to drive along. The worst thing for motorcyclists in particular is that they tend to hover about five feet, precisely visor height, from the ground.

I arrived in Jacksonville just in time to navigate the rush hour traffic around the city's busy ring road. As always, ten thousand temporary traffic cones had congregated there to narrow lanes, confuse drivers, and generally create mayhem. In all of my many visits to Jacksonville I had never once actually seen a construction worker within said roadworks. Not a single chap dressed like one of Village People, wearing a hard hat and a dayglo jacket and leaning on a shovel or doing something road worky. Local legend has it that Christ himself once navigated this section of road and was made exactly twenty-three minutes late for the last supper.

I found Paula in a Holiday Inn north of Jacksonville, located close to Mayport Naval Station where the aircraft carrier was scheduled to arrive in the morning. We went out for dinner and had a little walk along the broad stretch of golden sand of Atlantic Beach. The beach was pretty but Jacksonville, generally speaking, is not. It has the notoriously worst football team in the NFL, the Jacksonville Panthers. They were so appallingly bad, that speaking as somebody who cares not a whit, nor even understands the game, even I had heard of the Panthers. Jacksonville is almost somewhat notorious for its crippling crime rate and poverty. This, in a state already famous for its shootings and murder rates.

As if to prove a point, we retired to our hotel room to watch some TV before bed. We were both excited to see the aircraft carrier arrive and to see Ben sail away. I got into bed, butt naked, as was my custom, and we watched NSI or some other nonsense on the TV for a while.

As we watched, from far down the hall came a regular banging sound. It sounded like some kids were thumping on the bedroom doors and then running away. Time and again we heard the sound. Three staccato bangs on the door and then a long silence. The regular pattern slowly preceded down the hallway in our direction.

Finally, the banging rang out against our neighbour's door. I gave Paula an exasperated look of resignation and slipped out of bed to don my favourite batman budgie smugglers to wait our turn. I snuck in bare feet across the unnervingly tacky hotel carpet to stand behind the door.

I was good and riled up, and ready in wait for the kids to bang on our door, ready to swing the door open and give them a good piece of this unnecessarily disturbed English gentleman's mind.

Sure enough, silence ensued and then sixty seconds later, the expected, 'BANG, BANG, BANG'.

"Right. Got you, you little shits." I muttered.

I swung the door open and may have dribbled a little urine into my lucky underpants as, where I expected to find a couple of rascally teenagers, I now found myself staring into the cavernous business end of a tactical shotgun and the smaller but no less intimidating muzzle of a Glock.

Two uniformed officers stood there, eyes narrowed, fingers on triggers.

I slowly raised my hands and cleared the fear from my throat with a girlie croak. "How can I help you officers?" I managed.

"There has been a report of a weapon being discharged in the hotel. Did you hear anything?"

I muttered something about only just getting back to the hotel after being absent having just eaten a splendid dinner. For several heart pounding moments, they stood stock still, glaring at my expression as if to divine a falsehood. But then they peered around me to see the untidy room, cases and motorcycle gear thrown carelessly into a corner. Finally, they both stepped back and lowered weapons to look me up and down. They exchanged a tight little smile at the sight of my lucky underpants, and disappeared, to terrify the owners of the next room down the corridor.

In the morning, we had a quick breakfast in the hotel. I mentioned the night-time armed raid by Jacksonville's finest, but the receptionist just shrugged as if this was a regular occurrence and gave me a, "whaddaya want me to do about it, nobody got shot," eyebrow raise as she ran my credit card.

The Naval Station wasn't far, but we knew from visiting Pensacola that they can be vast, and security to gain entry can be difficult and time consuming.

We arrived at the security checkpoint in plenty of time and parked up to join the queue for the buses that whisk visiting relatives of sailors across the base to the pier where the aircraft carrier would soon arrive. A Military Policeman who could have been Jack Reacher's much bigger, steroid taking brother was checking names against the list. To get on the list the departing sailor had to submit his or her parent's details through the proper channels.

We had seen Ben only a day or so ago. We had discussed this entire scenario several times. Our confidence was high.

Reacher's brother walked across to us. He carried an M4 slung low under his left arm and had a nasty looking dagger tucked inside his bullet proof vest. He didn't look to me like he needed any additional weaponry at all. He looked like he could squeeze the life from me from ten feet away.

"Name."

"Wareing." I spelt it out to him slowly and carefully, aware that the name and spelling was always unfamiliar to an American ear.

"Uh, Uh."

"I beg your pardon?"

"Name aint on the list," he grunted.

I responded in an embarrassing falsetto. "Oh. Well, it should be. Our sailor, our son, Benjamin, is sailing from here this morning."

"Name aint on the list." He repeated.

My logic and well considered reasoning didn't seem to be having the intended effect.

"Perhaps you could check again?" I began to spell out the name again, "W A R E…"

"Name. Aint. On. The. List." He began to move away to the next parents in the long and quickly growing line.

"Wait!" I raised my voice and Reacher's eyebrows knotted in the manner that might crack a walnut from fifty paces.

"What I mean is…" I began.

I was luckily saved by a commanding officer, a captain I think, who must have overheard our dilemma. The captain walked over. He was tall and tanned and dressed in immaculate Navy whites, his gold braided cap tucked elegantly under one arm. I could almost hear the theme tune to 'An Officer and a Gentlemen,' playing in the background. The captain brushed an imaginary lock of jet-black hair from his steely grey eyes and ushered the incalcitrant man mountain away to intimidate other parents still waiting in line.

"What's the problem sir?" He said in a deep, smoke-tinged voice, the slightest hint of a Tennessee ascent, somehow adding both sex and sizzle to the whole interaction. I heard Paula giggle behind me.

"Our reliably unreliable son has somewhat forgotten to get our name on the list. We came all the way from Atlanta to see him off and now we can't get in to see him," I said.

"Well now. You good folks just give me a moment and I will see what I can do for y'all." He drawled in a voice that made even my knees buckle a little. Paula was drooling and wafting a hand in front of her reddening face.

He sauntered off, like John Wayne, in the direction of a little hut and we saw him pick up the phone and start to talk to somebody, presumably somebody even further up the chain of command.

As we waited, we saw the last of the visiting parents join the last waiting bus. The bus engine roared into life in a cloud of oily smoke and Reacher waved them through the security gate. The bus slowly disappeared into the distance.

Finally, after a good thirty minutes of anxious waiting the captain returned.

"I got permission for you good people to proceed."

"But the last bus has gone," said Paula.

He smiled, a row of perfect pearly white American dentistry, and Paula smiled back. I swear she fluttered her eyelids. She has never fluttered her eyelids. Not at me anyway.

To be fair, I had to admit, even to myself, he did look darn good in those navy whites.

"Well, ma'am, I can offer you a ride myself." He drawled.

I bet you can you smarmy Yank, I thought. But only to myself of course. We really needed a lift.

I expected the captain to own a Porsche or at least a flashy M-Series BMW so I was secretly thrilled to find that he drove a shit brown Honda Accord.

I might have been a foot shorter than him, with a slightly whiny British scouse tinted voice, and lacked both a hot uniform and any hair whatsoever. But I did own a motorcycle, God damn it. And motorcycles are cool.

The drive through the base took a long time. The facility was massive, and the roads were a complicated matrix that wove between mysterious warehouse type buildings that were only identified with numbers and letters, indecipherable to anybody not in the military.

The handsome captain dropped us off dockside. When he was gone Paula blushed and gushed, "Well, wasn't he the nicest man."

"Hmmmm," was all I could muster through my seething jealousy.

By the time we got to the pier, the aircraft carrier had already arrived. I was pissed. I really wanted to enjoy the whole experience. The band, the national anthem, the flyover by the F15s. By the time we got there, and the captain had let us out of his car, the fanfare, the pomp, and the spectacle were all over.

Crowds of white uniformed sailors were already streaming from arriving coaches. Weighed down by enormous kit bags they flowed in endless lines towards the waiting aircraft carrier.

The carrier itself was gigantic. It lay like a leviathan at the dock secured by hawsers twice as thick as the torso of any man. It brooded on the skyline; it dominated the horizon. It exuded militaristic brute force. Somehow the rust that cut through the flat grey paint added a hint of threat and capability. An ocean-going colossus.

We craned our necks to catch sight of Ben amidst the crowds, but it was a hopeless exercise. Just like at graduation in Great Lakes, the Navy had successfully turned its sailors into identical clones. All of a similar height, all with short, cropped hair, all dressed identically. They even moved and marched in the same way. We watched and waited until the last of them joined the ship, and then we waited even longer in the burning heat of the day to watch the ship first prepare for departure and then finally slip its lines.

The aircraft carrier U.S.S Ronald Reagan sounded its horns. Three long blasts that split the air, and then a veritable army of tugs busied themselves around her, like worker bees around a queen, to guide her away from the dock and into the sound that would lead her out towards the deep and broad Atlantic.

We scoured the decks for a last sight of Ben. Sailors lined the upper decks as the carrier moved slowly away from shore. But taking into account both the distance and the combined height of the ship it was probably close to a quarter of a mile away already, and the chances of getting a final, desperate glimpse of our son, and the hope of a last mutual wave of farewell were narrowing. And then, quite sadly, the odds reached a heart wrenching zero.

We turned to see that all of the buses, the ones booked and reserved for the parents who had received an invite from their sailors, the same sailors who had bothered to take the time to ensure that their parents would be on the list, had already departed.

Even the handsome fucking captain had left in his shitty Honda Accord.

We looked out past the now abandoned pier, out across the open water. The aircraft carrier was a deep purple silhouette, an increasingly small blur on the distant horizon. It was swiftly taking away our eldest son, whisking him away forever eastward. Even the planet seemed complicit in our separation, spinning him away, anti-clockwise, away from westward lands, home, and ourselves. Away from those who loved him, despite his occasional failings.

With a deep and mutual sigh, we turned our back on the disappearing carrier, and arm in arm, we took the first steps on the long, hot, and dusty walk back through the quickly emptying Naval base, back to the gate and then the long, lonely journey home.

We had our own farewells to plan and prepare for. The house was already under contract. Our possessions were up for sale on Facebook and a yard sale was scheduled for what remained.

Our time in the United States of America, that too was swiftly coming to an end. We would soon leave for Spain with just two suitcases each. We would start again in another country, learn another language, and try once again to integrate with yet another foreign culture.

It would be truly heart-wrenching to leave the USA, this idiosyncratic, maddening, joyful, wonderfully insular, belligerent, and boisterous country. We would always carry the gravity and gentle perennial embarrassment of our British beginnings, but in many, many ways, we had become Americans, and we would miss her forever.

And now I had to go and sell my bloody bike as well.

THE END.

Thank you so much for the read—it is genuinely appreciated. if you enjoyed the tale, it would be very

kind of you to leave a review on your favorite bookstore.

You can read the rest of the books in the series by clicking on the image below, or simply search Amazon for Andy C Wareing:

If you enjoyed these tales, do please check out my other books available on my website:

https://andycwareing.com/

ANDY C WAREING

Andy is a multi-genre Indie author, originally from the United Kingdom. He has lived with his wife Paula and their two dogs Archie and Pi in Atlanta GA for the last fifteen years (with the exception of a year in Spain/UK during the pandemic). At heart always British, he loved living in the U.S.A. but will never vocalize the American pronunciations of basil, banana, or tomato. He currently lives in leafy Somerset, a land of apples, cider, and weather so perpetually wet, 'wellies' are considered formal wear.

Please take a moment to visit my website to see more books and get great discounts and offers.

ANDY C WAREING

Be a stalker and follow me on Facebook, Goodreads, or my author page on Amazon for updates on new projects:

f
facebook.com/andycwareing

g
goodreads.com/author/show/21017809.Andy_C_Wareing

a
amazon.com/author/andycwareing

email: author@andycwareing.com